HBR'S 10 MUST READS

On
Platforms and Ecosystems

HBR's 10 Must Reads series is the definitive collection of ideas and best practices for aspiring and experienced leaders alike. These books offer essential reading selected from the pages of *Harvard Business Review* on topics critical to the success of every manager.

Titles include:

HBR's 10 Must Reads 2015
HBR's 10 Must Reads 2016
HBR's 10 Must Reads 2017
HBR's 10 Must Reads 2018
HBR's 10 Must Reads 2019
HBR's 10 Must Reads 2020
HBR's 10 Must Reads for CEOs
HBR's 10 Must Reads for New Managers
HBR's 10 Must Reads on AI, Analytics, and the New Machine Age
HBR's 10 Must Reads on Boards
HBR's 10 Must Reads on Building a Great Culture
HBR's 10 Must Reads on Business Model Innovation
HBR's 10 Must Reads on Change Management
HBR's 10 Must Reads on Collaboration
HBR's 10 Must Reads on Communication
HBR's 10 Must Reads on Design Thinking
HBR's 10 Must Reads on Diversity
HBR's 10 Must Reads on Emotional Intelligence
HBR's 10 Must Reads on Entrepreneurship and Startups
HBR's 10 Must Reads on Innovation
HBR's 10 Must Reads on Leadership
HBR's 10 Must Reads on Leadership (Vol. 2)
HBR's 10 Must Reads on Leadership for Healthcare
HBR's 10 Must Reads on Leadership Lessons from Sports
HBR's 10 Must Reads on Making Smart Decisions
HBR's 10 Must Reads on Managing Across Cultures
HBR's 10 Must Reads on Managing in a Downturn

On
Platforms
and
Ecosystems

HARVARD BUSINESS REVIEW PRESS
Boston, Massachusetts

Cataloging-in-Publication data is forthcoming.

ISBN: 978-1-63369-988-5
eISBN: 978-1-63369-989-2

The paper used in this publication meets the requirements of the American National Standard for Permanence of Paper for Publications and Documents in Libraries and Archives Z39.48-1992.

Contents

**HBR'S
10
MUST
READS**

On
Platforms and
Ecosystems

Pipelines, Platforms, and the New Rules of Strategy

by Marshall W. Van Alstyne, Geoffrey G. Parker, and Sangeet Paul Choudary

BACK IN 2007 the five major mobile-phone manufacturers—Nokia, Samsung, Motorola, Sony Ericsson, and LG—collectively controlled 90% of the industry's global profits. That year, Apple's iPhone burst onto the scene and began gobbling up market share.

By 2015 the iPhone *single-handedly* generated 92% of global profits, while all but one of the former incumbents made no profit at all.

How can we explain the iPhone's rapid domination of its industry? And how can we explain its competitors' free fall? Nokia and the others had classic strategic advantages that should have protected them: strong product differentiation, trusted brands, leading operating systems, excellent logistics, protective regulation, huge R&D budgets, and massive scale. For the most part, those firms looked stable, profitable, and well entrenched.

Certainly the iPhone had an innovative design and novel capabilities. But in 2007, Apple was a weak, nonthreatening player surrounded by 800-pound gorillas. It had less than 4% of market share in desktop operating systems and none at all in mobile phones.

As we'll explain, Apple (along with Google's competing Android system) overran the incumbents by exploiting the power of platforms and leveraging the new rules of strategy they give rise to. Platform businesses bring together producers and consumers in high-value exchanges. Their chief assets are information and interactions, which together are also the source of the value they create and their competitive advantage.

Understanding this, Apple conceived the iPhone and its operating system as more than a product or a conduit for services. It imagined them as a way to connect participants in two-sided markets—app developers on one side and app users on the other—generating value for both groups. As the number of participants on each side grew, that value increased—a phenomenon called "network effects," which is central to platform strategy. By January 2015 the company's App Store offered 1.4 million apps and had cumulatively generated $25 billion for developers.

Apple's success in building a platform business within a conventional product firm holds critical lessons for companies across industries. Firms that fail to create platforms and don't learn the new rules of strategy will be unable to compete for long.

Pipeline to Platform

Platforms have existed for years. Malls link consumers and merchants; newspapers connect subscribers and advertisers. What's changed in this century is that information technology has profoundly reduced the need to own physical infrastructure and assets. IT makes building and scaling up platforms vastly simpler and cheaper, allows nearly frictionless participation that strengthens network effects, and enhances the ability to capture, analyze, and exchange huge amounts of data that increase the platform's value to all. You don't need to look far to see examples of platform businesses, from Uber to Alibaba to Airbnb, whose spectacular growth abruptly upended their industries.

Though they come in many varieties, platforms all have an ecosystem with the same basic structure, comprising four types of players. The *owners* of platforms control their intellectual property and governance. *Providers* serve as the platforms' interface with users.

Idea in Brief

The Sea Change

Platform businesses that bring together producers and consumers, as Uber and Airbnb do, are gobbling up market share and transforming competition. Traditional businesses that fail to create platforms and to learn the new rules of strategy will struggle.

The New Rules

With a platform, the critical asset is the community and the resources of its members. The focus of strategy shifts from controlling to orchestrating resources, from optimizing internal processes to facilitating external interactions, and from increasing customer value to maximizing ecosystem value.

The Upshot

In this new world, competition can emerge from seemingly unrelated industries or from within the platform itself. Firms must make smart choices about whom to let onto platforms and what they're allowed to do there, and must track new metrics designed to monitor and boost platform interactions.

Producers create their offerings, and *consumers* use those offerings. (See the exhibit "The players in a platform ecosystem.")

To understand how the rise of platforms is transforming competition, we need to examine how platforms differ from the conventional "pipeline" businesses that have dominated industry for decades. Pipeline businesses create value by controlling a linear series of activities—the classic value-chain model. Inputs at one end of the chain (say, materials from suppliers) undergo a series of steps that transform them into an output that's worth more: the finished product. Apple's handset business is essentially a pipeline. But combine it with the App Store, the marketplace that connects app developers and iPhone owners, and you've got a platform.

As Apple demonstrates, firms needn't be only a pipeline or a platform; they can be both. While plenty of pure pipeline businesses are still highly competitive, when platforms enter the same marketplace, the platforms virtually always win. That's why pipeline giants such as Walmart, Nike, John Deere, and GE are all scrambling to incorporate platforms into their models.

The players in a platform ecosystem

A platform provides the infrastructure and rules for a marketplace that brings together producers and consumers. The players in the ecosystem fill four main roles but may shift rapidly from one role to another. Understanding the relationships both within and outside the ecosystem is central to platform strategy.

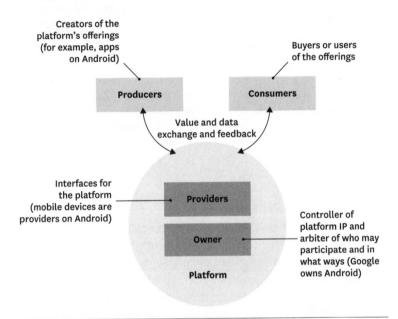

The move from pipeline to platform involves three key shifts:

1. From resource control to resource orchestration. The re-source-based view of competition holds that firms gain advantage by controlling scarce and valuable—ideally, inimitable—assets. In a pipeline world, those include tangible assets such as mines and real estate and intangible assets like intellectual property. With plat-forms, the assets that are hard to copy are the community and the resources its members own and contribute, be they rooms or cars

4

or ideas and information. In other words, the network of producers and consumers is the chief asset.

2. From internal optimization to external interaction. Pipeline firms organize their internal labor and resources to create value by optimizing an entire chain of product activities, from materials sourcing to sales and service. Platforms create value by facilitating interactions between external producers and consumers. Because of this external orientation, they often shed even variable costs of production. The emphasis shifts from dictating processes to persuading participants, and ecosystem governance becomes an essential skill.

3. From a focus on customer value to a focus on ecosystem value. Pipelines seek to maximize the lifetime value of individual customers of products and services, who, in effect, sit at the end of a linear process. By contrast, platforms seek to maximize the total value of an expanding ecosystem in a circular, iterative, feedback-driven process. Sometimes that requires subsidizing one type of consumer in order to attract another type.

These three shifts make clear that competition is more complicated and dynamic in a platform world. The competitive forces described by Michael Porter (the threat of new entrants and substitute products or services, the bargaining power of customers and suppliers, and the intensity of competitive rivalry) still apply. But on platforms these forces behave differently, and new factors come into play. To manage them, executives must pay close attention to the interactions on the platform, participants' access, and new performance metrics.

We'll examine each of these in turn. But first let's look more closely at network effects—the driving force behind every successful platform.

The Power of Network Effects

The engine of the industrial economy was, and remains, supply-side economies of scale. Massive fixed costs and low marginal costs mean that firms achieving higher sales volume than their competitors have a lower average cost of doing business. That allows them to reduce prices, which increases volume further, which permits more price cuts—a virtuous feedback loop that produces monopolies. Supply economics gave us Carnegie Steel, Edison Electric (which became GE), Rockefeller's Standard Oil, and many other industrial era giants.

In supply-side economies, firms achieve market power by controlling resources, ruthlessly increasing efficiency, and fending off challenges from any of the five forces. The goal of strategy in this world is to build a moat around the business that protects it from competition and channels competition toward other firms.

The driving force behind the internet economy, conversely, is demand-side economies of scale, also known as network effects. These are enhanced by technologies that create efficiencies in social networking, demand aggregation, app development, and other phenomena that help networks expand. In the internet economy, firms that achieve higher "volume" than competitors (that is, attract more platform participants) offer a higher average value per transaction. That's because the larger the network, the better the matches between supply and demand and the richer the data that can be used to find matches. Greater scale generates more value, which attracts more participants, which creates more value—another virtuous feedback loop that produces monopolies. Network effects gave us Alibaba, which accounts for over 75% of Chinese e-commerce transactions; Google, which accounts for 82% of mobile operating systems and 94% of mobile search; and Facebook, the world's dominant social platform.

The five forces model doesn't factor in network effects and the value they create. It regards external forces as "depletive," or extracting value from a firm, and so argues for building barriers against them. In demand-side economies, however, external forces can be "accretive"—adding value to the platform business. Thus the power of suppliers and customers, which is threatening in a supply-side world, may be viewed as an asset on platforms. Understanding when external forces may either add or extract value in an ecosystem is central to platform strategy.

How Platforms Change Strategy

In pipeline businesses, the five forces are relatively defined and stable. If you're a cement manufacturer or an airline, your customers and competitive set are fairly well understood, and the boundaries separating your suppliers, customers, and competitors are reasonably clear. In platform businesses, those boundaries can shift rapidly, as we'll discuss.

Forces within the ecosystem

Platform participants—consumers, producers, and providers—typically create value for a business. But they may defect if they believe their needs can be met better elsewhere. More worrisome, they may turn on the platform and compete directly with it. Zynga began as a games producer on Facebook but then sought to migrate players onto its own platform. Amazon and Samsung, providers of devices for the Android platform, tried to create their own versions of the operating system and take consumers with them.

The new roles that players assume can be either accretive or depletive. For example, consumers and producers can swap roles in ways that generate value for the platform. Users can ride with Uber today and drive for it tomorrow; travelers can stay with Airbnb one night and serve as hosts for other customers the next. In contrast, providers on a platform may become depletive, especially if they decide to compete with the owner. Netflix, a provider on the platforms of telecommunication firms, has control of consumers' interactions with the content it offers, so it can extract value from the platform owners while continuing to rely on their infrastructure.

As a consequence, platform firms must constantly encourage accretive activity within their ecosystems while monitoring participants' activity that may prove depletive. This is a delicate governance challenge that we'll discuss further.

Forces exerted by ecosystems

Managers of pipeline businesses can fail to anticipate platform competition from seemingly unrelated industries. Yet successful platform businesses tend to move aggressively into new terrain

Networks Invert the Firm

PIPELINE FIRMS HAVE LONG outsourced aspects of their internal functions, such as customer service. But today companies are taking that shift even further, moving toward orchestrating external networks that can complement or entirely replace the activities of once-internal functions.

Inversion extends outsourcing: Where firms might once have furnished design specifications to a known supplier, they now tap ideas they haven't yet imagined from third parties they don't even know. Firms are being turned inside out as value-creating activities move beyond their direct control and their organizational boundaries.

Marketing is no longer just about creating internally managed outbound messages. It now extends to the creation and propagation of messages by consumers themselves. Travel destination marketers invite consumers to submit videos of their trips and promote them on social media. The online eyeglasses retailer Warby Parker encourages consumers to post online photos of themselves modeling different styles and ask friends to help them choose. Consumers get more-flattering glasses, and Warby Parker gets viral exposure.

Information technology, historically focused on managing internal enterprise systems, increasingly supports external social and community networks. Threadless, a producer of T-shirts, coordinates communication not just to and from but among customers, who collaborate to develop the best product designs.

and into what were once considered separate industries with little warning. Google has moved from web search into mapping, mobile operating systems, home automation, driverless cars, and voice recognition. As a result of such shape-shifting, a platform can abruptly transform an incumbent's set of competitors. Swatch knows how to compete with Timex on watches but now must also compete with Apple. Siemens knows how to compete with Honeywell in thermostats but now is being challenged by Google's Nest.

Competitive threats tend to follow one of three patterns. First, they may come from an established platform with superior network effects that uses its relationships with customers to enter your industry. Products have features; platforms have communities, and those communities can be leveraged. Given Google's relation-

Human resources functions at companies increasingly leverage the wisdom of networks to augment internal talent. Enterprise software giant SAP has opened the internal system on which its developers exchange problems and solutions to its external ecosystem—to developers at both its own partners and its partners' clients. Information sharing across this network has improved product development and productivity and reduced support costs.

Finance, which historically has recorded its activities on private internal accounts, now records some transactions externally on public, or "distributed," ledgers. Organizations such as IBM, Intel, and JPMorgan are adopting blockchain technology that allows ledgers to be securely shared and vetted by anyone with permission. Participants can inspect everything from aggregated accounts to individual transactions. This allows firms to, for example, crowdsource compliance with accounting principles or seek input on their financial management from a broad network outside the company. Opening the books this way taps the wisdom of crowds and signals trustworthiness.

Operations and logistics traditionally emphasize the management of just-in-time inventory. More and more often, that function is being supplanted by the management of "not even mine" inventory—whether rooms, apps, or other assets owned by network participants. Indeed, if Marriott, Yellow Cab, and NBC had added platforms to their pipeline value chains, then Airbnb, Uber, and YouTube might never have come into being.

ship with consumers, the value its network provides them, and its interest in the internet of things, Siemens might have predicted the tech giant's entry into the home-automation market (though not necessarily into thermostats). Second, a competitor may target an overlapping customer base with a distinctive new offering that leverages network effects. Airbnb's and Uber's challenges to the hotel and taxi industries fall into this category. The final pattern, in which platforms that collect the same type of data that your firm does suddenly go after your market, is still emerging. When a data set is valuable, but different parties control different chunks of it, competition between unlikely camps may ensue. This is happening in health care, where traditional providers, producers of wearables like Fitbit, and retail pharmacies like Walgreens are all launching platforms based on the health data they own. They can be expected to compete for control of a broader data set—and the consumer relationships that come with it.

Focus

Managers of pipeline businesses focus on growing sales. For them, goods and services delivered (and the revenues and profits from them) are the units of analysis. For platforms, the focus shifts to interactions—exchanges of value between producers and consumers on the platform. The unit of exchange (say, a view of a video or a thumbs-up on a post) can be so small that little or no money changes hands. Nevertheless, the number of interactions and the associated network effects are the ultimate source of competitive advantage.

With platforms, a critical strategic aim is strong up-front design that will attract the desired participants, enable the right interactions (so-called core interactions), and encourage ever-more-powerful network effects. In our experience, managers often fumble here by focusing too much on the wrong type of interaction. And the perhaps counterintuitive bottom line, given how much we stress the importance of network effects, is that it's usually wise to ensure the value of interactions for participants before focusing on volume.

Most successful platforms launch with a single type of interaction that generates high value even if, at first, low volume. They then move into adjacent markets or adjacent types of interactions, increasing both value and volume. Facebook, for example, launched with a narrow focus (connecting Harvard students to other Harvard students) and then opened the platform to college students broadly and ultimately to everyone. LinkedIn launched as a professional networking site and later entered new markets with recruitment, publishing, and other offerings.

Access and governance

In a pipeline world, strategy revolves around erecting barriers. With platforms, while guarding against threats remains critical, the focus of strategy shifts to eliminating barriers to production and consumption in order to maximize value creation. To that end,

Harnessing Spillovers

POSITIVE SPILLOVER EFFECTS help platforms rapidly increase the volume of interactions. Book purchases on a platform, for example, generate book recommendations that create value for other participants on it, who then buy more books. This dynamic exploits the fact that network effects are often strongest among interactions of the same type (say, book sales) than among unrelated interactions (say, package pickup and yardwork in different cities mediated by the odd-job platform TaskRabbit).

Consider ride sharing. By itself, an individual ride on Uber is high value for both rider and driver—a desirable core interaction. As the number of platform participants increases, so does the value Uber delivers to both sides of the market; it becomes easier for consumers to get rides and for drivers to find fares. Spillover effects further enhance the value of Uber to participants: Data from riders' interactions with drivers—ratings of drivers and riders—improves the value of the platform to other users. Similarly, data on how well a given ride matched a rider's needs helps determine optimal pricing across the platform—another important spillover effect.

platform executives must make smart choices about access (whom to let onto the platform) and governance (or "control"—what consumers, producers, providers, and even competitors are allowed to do there).

Platforms consist of rules and architecture. Their owners need to decide how open both should be. An *open architecture* allows players to access platform resources, such as app developer tools, and create new sources of value. *Open governance* allows players other than the owner to shape the rules of trade and reward sharing on the platform. Regardless of who sets the rules, a fair reward system is key. If managers open the architecture but do not share the rewards, potential platform participants (such as app developers) have the ability to engage but no incentives. If managers open the rules and rewards but keep the architecture relatively closed, potential participants have incentives to engage but not the ability.

These choices aren't fixed. Platforms often launch with a fairly closed architecture and governance and then open up as they introduce new types of interactions and sources of value. But every platform must induce producers and consumers to interact and share their ideas and resources. Effective governance will inspire outsiders to bring valuable intellectual property to the platform, as Zynga did in bringing FarmVille to Facebook. That won't happen if prospective partners fear exploitation.

Some platforms encourage producers to create high-value offerings on them by establishing a policy of "permissionless innovation." They let producers invent things for the platform without approval but guarantee the producers will share in the value created. Rovio, for example, didn't need permission to create the Angry Birds game on the Apple operating system and could be confident that Apple wouldn't steal its IP. The result was a hit that generated enormous value for all participants on the platform. However, Google's Android platform has allowed even more innovation to flourish by being more open at the provider layer. That decision is one reason Google's market capitalization surpassed Apple's in early 2016 (just as Microsoft's did in the 1980s).

However, unfettered access can destroy value by creating "noise"—misbehavior or excess or low-quality content that inhibits interaction. One company that ran into this problem was Chatroulette, which paired random people from around the world for webchats. It grew exponentially until noise caused its abrupt collapse. Initially utterly open—it had no access rules at all—it soon encountered the "naked hairy man" problem, which is exactly what it sounds like. Clothed users abandoned the platform in droves. Chatroulette responded by reducing its openness with a variety of user filters.

Most successful platforms similarly manage openness to maximize positive network effects. Airbnb and Uber rate and insure hosts and drivers, Twitter and Facebook provide users with tools to prevent stalking, and Apple's App Store and the Google Play store both filter out low-quality applications.

Metrics

Leaders of pipeline enterprises have long focused on a narrow set of metrics that capture the health of their businesses. For example, pipelines grow by optimizing processes and opening bottlenecks;

one standard metric, inventory turnover, tracks the flow of goods and services through them. Push enough goods through and get margins high enough, and you'll see a reasonable rate of return.

As pipelines launch platforms, however, the numbers to watch change. Monitoring and boosting the performance of core interactions becomes critical. Here are new metrics managers need to track:

Interaction failure. If a traveler opens the Lyft app and sees "no cars available," the platform has failed to match an intent to consume with supply. Failures like these directly diminish network effects. Passengers who see this message too often will stop using Lyft, leading to higher driver downtimes, which can cause drivers to quit Lyft, resulting in even lower ride availability. Feedback loops can strengthen or weaken a platform.

Engagement. Healthy platforms track the participation of ecosystem members that enhances network effects—activities such as content sharing and repeat visits. Facebook, for example, watches the ratio of daily to monthly users to gauge the effectiveness of its efforts to increase engagement.

Match quality. Poor matches between the needs of users and producers weaken network effects. Google constantly monitors users' clicking and reading to refine how its search results fill their requests.

Negative network effects. Badly managed platforms often suffer from other kinds of problems that create negative feedback loops and reduce value. For example, congestion caused by unconstrained network growth can discourage participation. So can misbehavior, as Chatroulette found. Managers must watch for negative network effects and use governance tools to stem them by, for example, withholding privileges or banishing troublemakers.

Finally, platforms must understand the financial value of their communities and their network effects. Consider that in 2016, private equity markets placed the value of Uber, a demand economy firm founded in 2009, above that of GM, a supply economy firm founded in 1908. Clearly Uber's investors were looking beyond the traditional financials and metrics when calculating the firm's worth and potential. This is a clear indication that the rules have changed.

Because platforms require new approaches to strategy, they also demand new leadership styles. The skills it takes to tightly control internal resources just don't apply to the job of nurturing external ecosystems.

While pure platforms naturally launch with an external orientation, traditional pipeline firms must develop new core competencies—and a new mind-set—to design, govern, and nimbly expand platforms on top of their existing businesses. The inability to make this leap explains why some traditional business leaders with impressive track records falter in platforms. Media mogul Rupert Murdoch bought the social network Myspace and managed it the way he might have run a newspaper—from the top down, bureaucratically, and with a focus more on controlling the internal operation than on fostering the ecosystem and creating value for participants. In time the Myspace community dissipated and the platform withered.

The failure to transition to a new approach explains the precarious situation that traditional businesses—from hotels to health care providers to taxis—find themselves in. For pipeline firms, the writing is on the wall: Learn the new rules of strategy for a platform world, or begin planning your exit.

Originally published in April 2016. Reprint R1604C

Strategies for Two-Sided Markets

by Thomas Eisenmann, Geoffrey Parker, and Marshall W. Van Alstyne

IF YOU LISTED the blockbuster products and services that have redefined the global business landscape, you'd find that many of them tie together two distinct groups of users in a network. Case in point: What has been the most important innovation in financial services since World War II? Answer: almost certainly the credit card, which links consumers and merchants. Newspapers, HMOs, and computer operating systems also serve what economists call *two-sided markets* or *two-sided networks*. Newspapers, for instance, join subscribers and advertisers; HMOs link patients to a web of health care providers, and vice versa; operating systems connect computer users and application developers.

Products and services that bring together groups of users in two-sided networks are *platforms*. They provide infrastructure and rules that facilitate the two groups' transactions and can take many guises. In some cases, platforms rely on physical products, as with consumers' credit cards and merchants' authorization terminals. In other cases, they are places providing services, like shopping malls or websites such as Monster and eBay.

Two-sided networks can be found in many industries, sharing the space with traditional product and service offerings. However, two-sided networks differ from other offerings in a fundamental way. In the traditional value chain, value moves from left to right: To the left of the company is cost; to the right is revenue. In two-sided networks, cost and revenue are both to the left and the right, because the platform has a distinct group of users on each side. The platform incurs costs in serving both groups and can collect revenue from each, although one side is often subsidized, as we'll see.

The two groups are attracted to each other—a phenomenon that economists call the network effect. With two-sided network effects, the platform's value to any given user largely depends on the number of users on the network's other side. Value grows as the platform matches demand from both sides. For example, video game developers will create games only for platforms that have a critical mass of players, because developers need a large enough customer base to recover their upfront programming costs. In turn, players favor platforms with a greater variety of games.

Because of network effects, successful platforms enjoy increasing returns to scale. Users will pay more for access to a bigger network, so margins improve as user bases grow. This sets network platforms apart from most traditional manufacturing and service businesses. In traditional businesses, growth beyond some point usually leads to diminishing returns: Acquiring new customers becomes harder as fewer people, not more, find the firm's value proposition appealing.

Fueled by the promise of increasing returns, competition in two-sided network industries can be fierce. Platform leaders can leverage their higher margins to invest more in R&D or lower their prices, driving out weaker rivals. As a result, mature two-sided network industries are usually dominated by a handful of large platforms, as is the case in the credit card industry. In extreme situations, such as PC operating systems, a single company emerges as the winner, taking almost all of the market.

Platforms serving two-sided networks are not a new phenomenon. Energy companies and automakers, for example, link drivers of gasoline-powered cars and refueling stations in a well-established network. However, thanks largely to technology, platforms have become more prevalent in recent years. New platforms have been created (Google, for example, links advertisers and web searchers) and traditional businesses have been reconceived as platforms (for

Idea in Brief

If you listed the blockbuster offerings that have redefined the global business landscape, you'd find that many tie together two distinct groups of users. HMOs, for instance, link patients to health-care providers. Search engines join web surfers and advertisers.

When successful, these **platforms** catalyze a virtuous cycle: More demand from one user group spurs more from the other. For example, the more video games developers (one user group) create for the Microsoft Xbox platform, the more players (the other user group) snap up the latest Xbox. Meanwhile, the more players who use Xbox, the more developers willing to pay Microsoft a licensing fee to produce new games. And as user bases grow, margins fatten.

But as Eisenmann, Parker, and Van Alstyne contend, managing platforms is tricky: Strategies that make traditional offerings success-ful won't work in these two-sided markets. To capture the advan-tages that platforms promise, you must address three strategic challenges.

The key challenge? Get pric-ing right: "Subsidize" one user group while charging the other a premium for access to the sub-sidized group. Adobe's Acrobat PDF market comprises document readers and writers. Readers pay nothing for Acrobat software. Document producers, who prize this 500-million-strong audience, pay $299.

If you seize a platform opportunity but don't get it right the first time, someone else will. By mastering platforms' unique strategic chal-lenges, you'll gain a head start over your competition.

instance, retail electricity markets are evolving into platforms that match consumers with specific power producers, allowing them to express their preferences for cheaper coal or more costly renewable power). Yet for all the potential they've spotted, platform providers have struggled to establish and sustain their two-sided networks. Their failures are rooted in a common mistake. In creating strategies for two-sided networks, managers have typically relied on assump-tions and paradigms that apply to products *without* network effects. As a result, they have made many decisions that are wholly inappro-priate for the economics of their industries.

In the following article, we draw on recent theoretical work[1] to guide executives in negotiating the challenges of two-sided

Idea in Practice

To ensure your platform's success:

Get Pricing Right

Consider these pricing strategies:

- **Subsidize quality- and price-sensitive users.** For example, if PDF document *readers* were charged even a tiny amount, Adobe Acrobat Reader's immense user base would be much smaller, reducing document *producers'* interest and their willingness to pay a premium for access to readers. Readers, much more price sensitive than document producers, wouldn't pay for access to a bigger base of writers.

- **Secure "marquee" users' exclusive participation in your platform.** Providing incentives for marquee users (for instance, anchor stores in a mall) to participate exclusively in your platform (the mall) can attract more users from the other user group (retailers who lease space in malls with prestigious anchor stores). Result? Your platform's growth accelerates.

Cope with Winner-Take-All Competition

The prospect of fat margins in two-sided markets can fuel an intense desire among rivals to become the *only* platform provider. To deal with the competition:

- **Decide whether the two-sided market you're eyeing will eventually be served by a single platform.** The answer's "Yes" if using more than one comparable platform would be costly to users and if special features don't increase value to users.

Example: The DVD industry meets these criteria: Owning multiple DVD players would be expensive for consumers; providing multiple formats, costly for movie studios. And DVD players don't lend themselves to

networks. We begin by looking at the factors that senior managers must consider in designing their platforms' business models. The key decision here is pricing. As we've noted, providers of platforms for two-sided networks are able to draw revenue from both sides. In most cases, though, it makes sense to subsidize certain users. The crucial strategy question is, Which side should you subsidize, and for how long?

The next step is to figure out how to manage winner-take-all dynamics. Many two-sided network industries are served almost distinctive features, since they connect to TV sets that would negate any DVD player's unique picture and sound capabilities.

- **Decide whether to share the single platform or fight for proprietary control.** Sharing has benefits: Total market size expands and rivalry lessens, reducing market outlays. That's why DVD industry contenders opted to pool their technologies. They jointly created the DVD format in 1995, avoiding a replay of the costly video players' VHS-Beta standards clash.

Want to fight for proprietary control? You'll need deep pockets, a reputation for past prowess, and preexisting relationships with prospective users. When launching Acrobat, for instance, Adobe marketed to its existing user base for PostScript printing products.

Avoid Envelopment

Many platforms have overlapping user groups, tempting some related platform providers to swallow others' users. Mobile phones, for instance, now incorporate music and video players, PCs, and credit cards. To avoid being swallowed, consider changing your business model.

Example: Under attack from Microsoft, RealNetworks (which pioneered streaming media software) ceded the streaming media business. It leveraged existing relationships with consumers and music companies to launch Rhapsody—a $10-per-month subscription music service that offers unlimited streaming to any PC from a library of a half-million songs. It now profits from consumers versus subsidizing them.

entirely by a single platform. In some cases, just one company controls that platform, as with eBay's auctions or Microsoft's Windows. In other cases, multiple companies share the dominant platform, as with DVD and fax standards or, in real estate, a regional multiple listing service. (See the sidebar "Examples of Two-Sided Networks.") When a network industry is likely to be served by a single platform, aspiring providers must make a "bet the company" decision. Should they fight to gain proprietary control over the platform or share the spoils with rivals?

Platform providers that have vanquished their immediate rivals can't rest on their laurels. Indeed, they face a significant competitive threat from large companies operating in adjacent markets that have the ability to offer a multiplatform bundle. In our final section, we explore this challenge and offer prescriptions for firms that face it. As we'll see, moving first and getting big quickly aren't necessarily the right answers.

Challenge 1: Pricing the Platform

In competitive industries, prices are largely determined by the marginal cost of producing an extra unit, and margins tend to be thin. In industries with high barriers to entry, the price ceiling is set by customers' willingness to pay, and margins are more likely to be fat.

For two-sided networks, pricing is a more complicated affair. Platform providers have to choose a price for each side, factoring in the impact on the other side's growth and willingness to pay. Typically, two-sided networks have a "subsidy side," that is, a group of users who, when attracted in volume, are highly valued by the "money side," the other user group. Because the number of subsidy-side users is crucial to developing strong network effects, the platform provider sets prices for that side below the level it would charge if it viewed the subsidy side as an independent market. Conversely, the money side pays more than it would if it were viewed as an independent market. The goal is to generate "cross-side" network effects: If the platform provider can attract enough subsidy-side users, money-side users will pay handsomely to reach them. Cross-side network effects also work in the reverse direction. The presence of money-side users makes the platform more attractive to subsidy-side users, so they will sign up in greater numbers. The challenge for the platform provider with pricing power on both sides is to determine the degree to which one group should be encouraged to swell through subsidization and how much of a premium the other side will pay for the privilege of gaining access to it.

Examples of Two-Sided Networks

INSIGHTS ABOUT THE ECONOMICS of two-sided networks apply to a variety of industries. In cases where platforms—the products and sevices that bring together groups of users—are proprietary, there invariably is a clear subsidy side and a clear money side. For example, doctors—in exchange for access to a higher volume of patients—agree to rates below those they could command if they were not affiliated with an HMO.

Networks served by shared platforms tend to lack a subsidy side. It is hard for platform providers to recover subsidies if rivals share the fees collected from the network's money side. Real estate brokers avoid this free-rider problem by splitting the seller's fee 50/50. Subsidies also disappear when a shared platform's providers do not have pricing power on both sides of the network, as in the case of gasoline-powered transportation.

Networked market	Side 1	Side 2	Platform providers
			Rival providers of proprietary platforms
PC operating systems	Consumers	Application developers*	Windows, Macintosh
Online recruitment	Job seekers*	Employers	Monster, CareerBuilder
Miami Yellow Pages	Consumers*	Advertisers	BellSouth, Verizon
Web search	Searchers*	Advertisers	Google, Yahoo
HMOs	Patients*	Doctors	Kaiser, WellPoint
Video games	Players*	Developers	PlayStation, Xbox
Minneapolis shopping malls	Shoppers*	Retailers	Mall of America, Southdale Center
			Rival providers of shared platforms
Linux application servers	Enterprises	Application developers	IBM, Hewlett-Packard, Dell
Wi-Fi equipment	Laptop users	Access points	Linksys, Cisco, Dell
DVD	Consumers	Studios	Sony, Toshiba, Samsung
Phoenix Realtors Association	Home buyers*	Home sellers	100+ real estate brokerage firms
Gasoline-powered engines	Auto owners	Fueling stations	GM, Toyota, Exxon, Shell
Universal Product Code	Product suppliers	Retailers	NCR, Symbol Technologies

* Denotes network's subsidy side

Pricing is further complicated by "same-side" network effects, which are created when drawing users to one side helps attract even more users to that side. For example, as more people buy PlayStation consoles, new users will find it easier to trade games with friends or find partners for online play. Economists call this snowballing pattern a positive same-side network effect. (Same-side network effects can also be negative. For a more detailed explanation of how network effects attract or deter users, see the sidebar "The Dynamics of Two-Sided Networks.")

It is not always obvious which side—if either—the platform should subsidize and which it should charge. During the dot-com boom, for example, nascent B2B exchanges agonized over whether to charge fees to buyers, sellers, or both, and how charges should be split between fixed subscription payments and variable transaction fees. (See the sidebar "Similar Networks, Different Pricing" for an illustration of how two seemingly similar networks may require very different pricing strategies.)

To make the right decisions about pricing, executives of platform providers need to look closely at the following factors:

Ability to capture cross-side network effects

Your giveaway will be wasted if your network's subsidy side can transact with a rival platform provider's money side. That's what happened to Netscape, which subsidized its browser to individuals in the hope of selling web servers to companies operating websites. However, website operators didn't have to buy Netscape's server in order to send pages to Netscape's big base of users; they could buy a rival's web server instead.

User sensitivity to price

Generally, it makes sense to subsidize the network's more price-sensitive side and to charge the side that increases its demand more strongly in response to the other side's growth. Adobe's Acrobat software follows this pricing rule. Acrobat presents any electronic document in Portable Document Format (PDF), a universal standard that can be printed or viewed exactly as it appeared in its original

The Dynamics of Two-Sided Networks

TRANSACTIONS IN TWO-SIDED NETWORKS always entail a triangular set of relationships. Two user groups—the network's "sides"—interact with each other through one or more intermediaries called *platform providers*. A *platform* embodies an *architecture*—a design for products, services, and infrastructure facilitating network users' interactions—plus a set of *rules;* that is, the protocols, rights, and pricing terms that govern transactions. These platforms exhibit two types of network effects, which may be either positive or negative: A same-side effect, in which increasing the number of users on one side of the network makes it either more or less valuable to users on the same side; and a cross-side effect, in which increasing the number of users on one side of the network makes it either more or less valuable to the users on the other side. Cross-side network effects are typically positive, but they can be negative (TV viewers preferring fewer ads). Same-side network effects are often negative (sellers preferring fewer rivals in a B2B exchange), but they may be positive (Microsoft Xbox owners valuing the fact that they can play games with friends).

application. The PDF network consists of two sets of users—writers, who create documents, and readers, who view them—using different software. Readers are very price sensitive; they pay nothing for their software. If readers were charged even a small amount, Adobe Reader's 500-million-person user base would be much smaller. Writers, who greatly value this huge audience, pay a fee for their software. If Adobe reversed its approach, charging readers and subsidizing writers, its network would collapse. Writers are less price sensitive, so free software would not dramatically boost their numbers. More to the point, readers would not pay much for access to a bigger base of writers.

User sensitivity to quality
High sensitivity to quality also marks the side you should subsidize. This pricing prescription can be counterintuitive: Rather than charge the side that strongly *demands* quality, you charge the side that must *supply* quality. Such a strategy is evident in video games. To deliver compelling quality, game developers incur enormous fixed costs. To amortize these costs, they must be assured that the platform has many users. Hence the need for a consumer subsidy.

Similar Networks, Different Pricing

ON FIRST INSPECTION, PC and video game networks look similar. In both cases, end users on one side wishing to link to software or games on the other side buy a platform consisting of an operating system (OS) bundled with hardware—a PC or a game console. The two businesses exhibit similarly positive cross-side network effects: End users favor platforms that offer a wide variety of complements. Developers favor platforms with more end users because this improves the odds that they will recover the fixed, upfront costs of creating complements.

Notwithstanding these similarities, the PC and game industries use very different pricing models. In video games, end users are subsidized. Platform providers like Sony PlayStation and Microsoft Xbox historically have priced consoles at or below cost. Game developers are on the network's money side; they pay a royalty to console manufacturers of as much as 20% of a game's retail price. In the PC industry, the money side and subsidy side are reversed. End users are the money side, paying well above cost for the platform's essential element—its OS—which comes bundled with PCs offered by OEMs like Gateway. Application developers are the subsidy side. They pay no royalties and receive free software development kits from the OS vendors.

Why do these similar two-sided networks have fundamentally different pricing structures? Video game console users—typically teenagers—are both far more price sensitive and quality conscious than typical PC users. On average,

Platform providers make sure game developers meet high quality standards by imposing strict licensing terms and charging a high royalty. This "tax" is not passed through to consumers: Developers charge the highest prices the market will bear, regardless of the royalty rate. However, the royalty helps weed out games of marginal quality. Once the "tax" is added, titles with poor sales prospects cannot generate enough contribution margin to cover their fixed costs, so they never get made in the first place.

Output costs
Pricing decisions are more straightforward when each new subsidy-side user costs the platform provider essentially nothing.

each console owner buys just eight games, which cost about $50 apiece. Over the two- to three-year life of a console, these precious titles are consumed sequentially in intense bursts; gamers spend a great deal of time—40 to 100 hours—with each title.

To deliver compelling quality, game developers incur enormous fixed costs. To amortize these costs, they must be assured that the console has many users: Hence the need for a consumer subsidy. Console providers police quality by imposing strict licensing terms and charging a high royalty. This "tax," absorbed by the developers, helps weed out games of marginal quality. Developers cannot afford to offer titles with weak sales prospects, once the tax is added to their price.

By contrast, PCs are often purchased for work and are otherwise more likely viewed as household necessities than game consoles are, so price sensitivity is lower. Over their lives, PCs accumulate scores of applications, ranging from the indispensable (such as word processing) to the disposable (for example, some casual games). Accordingly, we observe a huge range of price and quality levels for applications.

It's true that both PC users and gamers value variety and quality and that developers in both networks value the ability to reach a large installed base. However, gamers' need for quality seems to be stronger, as does game developers' need for large numbers of consumers.

This will be the case when the giveaway takes the form of a digital good such as a software program or a cheap service such as otherwise-idle computer time. However, when a giveaway product has appreciable unit costs, as with tangible goods, platform providers must be more careful. If a strong willingness to pay does not materialize on the money side, a giveaway strategy with high variable costs can quickly rack up large losses. FreePC learned this lesson in 1999 when it provided computers and internet access at no cost to consumers who agreed to view internet-delivered ads that could not be minimized or hidden. Unfortunately, few marketers were eager to target consumers who were so cost conscious. FreePC abandoned its offer after incurring $80 million in losses.

Same-side network effects

Surprisingly, sometimes it makes sense to deliberately exclude some users from the network. Platform providers normally welcome growth in the user base on either side, because it encourages growth on the other side. In addition to positive cross-side network effects, however, platform managers must assess the possibility of negative same-side network effects, which can be quite strong. In most markets, sellers would be happy to see fewer direct rivals; the same can be true for buyers when goods are scarce. For example, many auto parts manufacturers, concerned about downward pricing pressure, refused to participate in Covisint, a B2B exchange organized by auto manufacturers. Covisint stalled, as did many other B2B market makers that failed to recruit enough sellers. In the face of strongly negative same-side network effects, platform providers should consider granting exclusive rights to a single user in each transaction category—and extracting high rent for this concession. The platform manager then must make sure that sellers do not abuse their monopoly positions; otherwise, buyers will avoid the network. Online car-buying services like Autobytel, which forwards consumers' queries to a single dealer in any given geographic territory, have succeeded with this strategy. Autobytel has earned a modest profit over the past three years; more to the point, it survived the dot-com crash that extinguished many internet market makers with flawed strategies.

Users' brand value

All users of two-sided networks are not created equal. The participation of "marquee users" can be especially important for attracting participants to the other side of the network. Marquee users may be exceptionally big buyers, like the U.S. government. Or they may be high-profile suppliers, like anchor stores in malls. A platform provider can accelerate its growth if it can secure the exclusive participation of marquee users in the form of a commitment from them not to join rival platforms. For many years, this kind of exclusive arrangement was at the core of Visa's marketing campaigns (". . . and they don't take American Express"). Of course, it can be expensive—especially for small platforms—to convince marquee users to forfeit opportunities in other networks. When the participation of a few large users is crucial for mobilizing a network, conflict over the division of value between platform providers and large users is common. Microsoft learned this when Electronic Arts (EA)—the largest developer of video games and thus a major potential money-side user of Microsoft's Xbox platform—refused to create online, multiplayer versions of its games for the Xbox Live service. EA objected to Microsoft's refusal to share subscription fees from Xbox Live, among other issues. After an 18-month stalemate, EA finally agreed to offer Xbox Live games. Terms of the agreement were not made public, but at the time, Microsoft announced that it would halt the in-house development of new games that would compete with EA's flagship sports titles.

Failing to recognize that two-sided network pricing follows different rules than conventional businesses can sink even the most attractive platforms. Apple provides a cautionary tale about misapplied pricing logic. Apple's well-regarded Macintosh operating system has always commanded a price premium from consumers. When it launched the Mac, Apple also tried to extract rent from the other side of its network, charging third-party developers $10,000 for the software development kits (SDKs) required to create Macintosh applications. By contrast, Microsoft gave Windows SDKs away for free. Tellingly, by the time of Microsoft's antitrust trial, Windows had six times as many applications as Macintosh. This made Windows far more attractive to consumers, despite its functional shortcomings.

Challenge 2: Winner-Take-All Dynamics

The prospect of increasing returns to scale in network industries can lead to winner-take-all battles, so an aspiring platform provider must consider whether to share its platform with rivals or fight to the death. Companies sometimes get this decision wrong, as with Sony's futile battle to establish its Betamax videocassette standard.

Coping with platform competition is a two-step process. First, executives must determine whether their networked market is destined to be served by a single platform. When this is the case, the second step—deciding whether to fight or share the platform—is a bet-the-company decision. The stakes are much higher when a networked market has room for fewer rival platforms.

Turning to the first step, a networked market is likely to be served by a single platform when the following three conditions apply:

- *Multi-homing costs are high for at least one user side.* "Homing" costs comprise all the expenses network users incur—including adoption, operation, and the opportunity cost of time—in order to establish and maintain platform affiliation. When users make a "home" on multiple platforms, they increase their outlays accordingly. For example, the vast majority of PC users rely on a single operating system—almost always Windows—because using multiple operating systems is expensive in terms of the additional hardware, software, and training required. Similarly, distance limits the number of shopping malls that consumers can visit at any one time, which in turn limits the number of malls. When multi-homing costs are high, users need a good reason to affiliate with multiple platforms.

- *Network effects are positive and strong—at least for the users on the side of the network with high multi-homing costs.* When cross-side network effects are positive and strong, those network users will tend to converge on one platform. A small-scale platform will be of little interest to users unless it is the only way to reach certain users on the other side. The odds of a single platform prevailing also increase when same-side network effects are positive: for example, when users of a software program need to share files with one another.

- *Neither side's users have a strong preference for special features.* If certain users have unique needs, then smaller, differentiated platforms can focus on those needs and carve out niches in a larger rival's shadow. American Express, for example, earns high margins despite having issued only 5% as many credit cards as Visa. American Express cards have no preset spending limit—a valuable feature for business travelers, made possible because cardholders must pay their full balance every month. Visa cannot match this feature, because the loans it extends to cardholders put an upper limit on their spending. In cases where special features are not important, however, users will tend to converge on a single platform.

The DVD industry meets these three conditions. First, multi-homing costs are high for consumers because it would be expensive to buy multiple players. Likewise, multi-homing costs are high for studios: Having to provide the same content in multiple incompatible formats would increase inventories and distribution costs. Second, cross-side network effects are strong for both sides of the network. Most consumers value access to a wide variety of titles, and studios realize scale economies when they can sell to more consumers. Third, opportunities for technical differentiation are modest, because DVD players connect to TV sets, which are standardized in ways that intrinsically limit DVD picture and sound quality.

For these reasons, the DVD market was bound to be served by a single platform. Potential platform providers anticipated this outcome and faced a choice: They could fight for proprietary control of the platform or pool their technologies. Industry participants chose the latter approach, jointly creating the DVD format in 1995 and avoiding a replay of the VHS-Betamax standards battle.

Why share a network when proprietary control promises monopoly profits once rivals are vanquished? The answer seems clear enough if senior managers believe that their company's platform is not likely to prevail. However, even those firms that have a fighting chance of gaining proprietary control stand to realize benefits from sharing. First, the total market size will be greater with a shared platform. During a battle for dominance in a two-sided network, some users will delay adoption, fearing that they will be stranded with obsolete investments—like a Betamax VCR—if they back the loser. Second, since the stakes are so high in battles for network dominance, firms spend enormous amounts on up-front marketing. Rivalry tends to be less intense with a shared platform, reducing marketing outlays.

Winning the battle

To fight successfully, you will need, at a minimum, cost or differentiation advantages. Three other assets are important in establishing proprietary control: First, platform providers gain an edge when they have preexisting relationships with prospective users—often in related businesses. Adobe, for example, leveraged its user base for PostScript printing products when launching PDF. Second, high expectations generate momentum in platform wars, so a reputation for past prowess helps a great deal. Having vanquished rival PC operating systems, Microsoft is feared and respected as a ruthless and competent rival. Third, in a war of attrition, deep pockets matter. Again, just ask Microsoft!

First-mover advantages can also be significant in platform battles, but they are not always decisive. In fact, when the market evolves slowly, late mover advantages may be more salient. Late movers may, for example, avoid the pioneer's positioning errors, be better placed to incorporate the latest technology into product designs, or be able to reverse engineer pioneers' products and beat them on cost. Google, which lagged web-search pioneers by several years, avoided portals' clutter in favor of a simple, fast-loading home page. It also copied and then improved on Overture's paid-listing model for generating revenue from searches.

In a battle for platform control, first and late movers alike will feel strong pressure to amass users as quickly as possible. In most cases, this urgency is appropriate. Positive word-of-mouth favors the early mover. But racing to acquire users can be a mistake under two circumstances. First, executives must ask whether their business is readily scalable. For example, platforms that must support complex customer-service interactions—like stop-loss orders or margin trades at an online brokerage firm—typically require skilled professionals. The need to recruit and train such personnel can put the brakes on rapid growth. Second, due to their explosive growth potential, platform-mediated networks are prone to boom or bust valuation cycles. When they launch cash-draining "get big fast" strategies, therefore, top managers need to be sure that funding will be forthcoming should capital-market sentiment turn negative.

Challenge 3: The Threat of Envelopment

You can do a great job addressing pricing and winner-take-all challenges and establish a successful new platform yet still face great danger. Why? Your platform may be "enveloped" by an adjacent platform provider that enters your market. Platforms frequently have overlapping user bases. Leveraging these shared relationships can make it easy and attractive for one platform provider to swallow the network of another. The real damage comes when your new rival offers your platform's functionality as part of a multiplatform bundle. Such bundling hurts the stand-alone platform provider when its money side perceives that a rival's bundle delivers more functionality at a lower total price. The stand-alone platform provider cannot respond to this value proposition because it cannot afford to cut the price on its money side and it cannot assemble a comparable bundle.

Networked markets—especially those in which technology is evolving rapidly—are rich with envelopment opportunities that can blur market boundaries. This blurring is called "convergence." For example, mobile phones now incorporate the functionality of music and video players, PCs, and even credit cards. Likewise, eBay—having acquired PayPal and the voice-over-internet protocol (VoIP) start-up Skype, as well as equity in Craigslist—is on a collision course with Google, which also offers a payment service (Google Checkout), VoIP (Google Talk), and a listing service (Google Base).

In many cases, a stand-alone business facing envelopment has little choice but to sell out to the attacker or exit the field. Some, however, manage to survive. RealNetworks, the pioneer of streaming media software, is—at least so far—a case in point.

Real's original business model was ideally suited to the needs of its two-sided network: Consumers downloaded its streaming media player for free, and content companies paid for its server software. As a result, the company quickly dominated the new market and earned modest profits in 1999 and 2000. But as early as 1998, Real's streaming media franchise was under attack from Microsoft. Like Real, Microsoft freely supplied its Windows Media Player (WMP) to consumers. But Microsoft also bundled its streaming software at no additional cost as a standard feature of its NT Server—a multipurpose operating system that also incorporated file, print, e-mail, and web servers, among other functions.

Since content companies—Real's money side—needed a multipurpose server anyway, they could buy NT and receive a "free" streaming media server. As content companies embraced this attractive proposition, consumers switched with them, because Microsoft's streaming media servers worked only with its own media players, and vice versa. By 2003, 42% of internet users in North America identified WMP as their primary media player, compared with 19% for Real's player.

Microsoft has not been the only threat. Real's Rhapsody subscription music service is now threatened with envelopment by Yahoo and ultimately by Apple. In 2005, Yahoo introduced a subscription music service—including downloads to portable music players—for $5 per month. Yahoo could afford to price aggressively, because bundling subscription music into its portal would increase user retention rates and, through cross-marketing, boost revenue from its other services. Likewise, Apple might choose to offer a subscription version of iTunes, drawing on the very lucrative iPod—its money side—to subsidize an envelopment attack. Real cannot match it rivals' bundles because it does not own a portal or sell an MP3 player.

But Real is not without options. Its defense against Microsoft and, more recently, Yahoo and Apple shows what a focused firm can do to survive envelopment.

Change business models

Real's response to Microsoft's envelopment attack was to switch its money side. Ceding the streaming media business, Real leveraged existing relationships with consumers and music companies to launch Rhapsody in 2003, charging $10 per month for unlimited streaming to any PC from a library of a half-million songs. Real now profited from consumers, rather than subsidizing them. Another common way for specialists like Real to reinvigorate their business models is to offer services as a systems integrator—helping enterprises knit together diverse systems and technologies. Indeed, Real was doing precisely that for a number of big music companies even before it launched Rhapsody. And it's no accident that IBM—the dominant provider of computing platforms through the mid-1980s—has more recently focused on systems integration. Facilitating transactions across a two-sided network requires platform providers to coordinate users' activities. Hence, managing a platform builds system integration skills that can be exploited.

Find a "bigger brother"

When bullied on the playground, a little guy needs a big friend. Real has found allies through partnerships with cable TV system operators and cellular phone companies. Subscription music—which requires a broadband connection—makes cable modem service stickier: Once consumers commit to a music service, they face switching costs. Changing vendors would force them to configure new music players and recreate playlists. Real also bundles its Rhapsody internet radio product with Sprint's wireless phone service and streaming video with Cingular's service. Cellular phone companies are attractive allies for Real, because they can mount their own envelopment attacks if Apple ever enters the subscription music market. Cellular carriers can afford to subsidize digital music playback on their phones, since doing so would be likely to reduce cell phone churn rates. That would present a big threat to Apple's money side.

Sue

Firms facing envelopment are wise to consider legal remedies, because antitrust law for two-sided networks is still in dispute. Antitrust law was conceived to constrain the behavior of traditional manufacturing firms and does not fully reflect the economic imperatives of platform-mediated networks. For this reason, dominant platform providers that offer bundles or pursue penetration pricing run the risk of being charged with illegal tying or predation. Exploiting this opportunity, Real brought Microsoft to antitrust court and then in 2005 received a $760 million payment from Microsoft to end the lawsuit. Sun Microsystems and Time Warner—Netscape's current owner—reaped similar bounties after they challenged Microsoft's anticompetitive behavior in court.

The threat of envelopment means that vigilance is crucial for a focused platform provider. Formulating strategy for platform-mediated networks is like playing three-dimensional chess: When market boundaries blur, envelopment attacks can come from any direction. However, focused firms are not without advantages when competing with large, diversified companies. Big firms can be slow to recognize envelopment opportunities and even slower to mobilize resources to exploit them. Also, envelopment requires cross-business-unit cooperation, a significant barrier in many diversified companies. Sony, for example, has struggled to coordinate strategy across its consumer electronics, video game, movie, and music businesses. Once the industry's trailblazer with products like the Walkman, Sony has seen Apple usurp this role. Mistakes like this on the part of established companies are precisely why former upstarts like Google, eBay, and Yahoo have grown into giants.

Despite the ubiquity of network industries and the attractions of owning a successful platform, the strategic implications of two-sided networks have gone largely unexplored. In the past, this lack of understanding was less problematic because executives usually had the luxury of formulating strategies for two-sided networks through trial and error. Markets today are less forgiving. Many opportunities for platform creation arise in high-tech sectors with short product life cycles. Opportunities also abound in traditional industries reconceived as two-sided networks. And, thanks to the internet, firms have easy access to both sides of new markets. In this environment, if you draw attention to a platform opportunity and don't get it right the first time, someone else will. Thinking carefully through the strategic issues we've outlined here will give you a head start.

Originally published in October 2006. Reprint R0610F

Note

1. See Geoffrey Parker and Marshall W. Van Alstyne, "Two-Sided Networks: A Theory of Information Product Design," *Management Science* (2005) and Jean-Charles Rochet and Jean Tirole, "Platform Competition in Two-Sided Markets," *Journal of the European Economic Association* (2003).

Finding the Platform in Your Product

by Andrei Hagiu and Elizabeth J. Altman

FIVE OF THE TEN MOST VALUABLE COMPANIES in the world today—Apple, Alphabet, Amazon, Facebook, and Microsoft—derive much of their worth from their multisided platforms (MSPs), which facilitate interactions or transactions between parties. Many MSPs are more valuable than companies in the same industries that provide only products or services: For instance, Airbnb is now worth more than Marriott, the world's largest hotel chain.

However, companies that weren't born as platform businesses rarely realize that they can—at least partially—turn their products and services into an MSP. And even if they do realize it, they often wander in the dark searching for a strategy to achieve this transformation. Here we provide a framework for doing so. It lays out four specific ways in which products and services can be turned into platforms and examines the strategic advantages and pitfalls of each. These ideas are applicable to physical as well as online businesses.

Why seek to transform products and services into MSPs in the first place? As one Intuit executive told us, it comes down to "fear and greed." Greed, of course, refers to the potential for new revenue sources that could speed growth and increase a company's value. Fear refers to the danger that existing and incoming competitors will steal market share from your product or service. Transforming an offering into a platform might enhance your company's competitive advantage and raise barriers to entry via network effects and higher switching costs. We're not suggesting that every company should try to emulate Airbnb, Alibaba, Facebook, or Uber. But many companies would benefit from adding elements of a platform business to their offerings.

Our goal is to help managers discern how their products or services could become multisided platforms—and what challenges and opportunities might arise—so that they can decide whether or not to make the change. Our framework derives from our combined experience studying and advising more than a dozen companies (including several mentioned below) during product-to-MSP transformations. Managers might want to use this article as the basis for a corporate-strategy offsite at which everyone is given the task of articulating MSP strategies around existing company offerings. That assignment should include answering questions such as: (1) Are there benefits to turning some or all of our products and services into MSPs? (2) Are there risks involved in doing so? (3) What key resources, relationships (including how we interact with customers), and organizational changes would be required for such a transformation?

The reason regular products and services are not multisided platforms is that they do not serve multiple groups or facilitate interactions between customers or groups. In this article we discuss four ways in which regular products and services can bridge this gap and become MSPs.

1. Opening the Door to Third Parties

In this scenario your product or service has a big customer base that third-party sellers of other offerings are interested in reaching. You become an MSP by making it possible for those third parties to connect with your customers. "Connect with" can mean advertise or sell (or both) to them. The third-party products may be independent of your product or service or may be apps or modules that work in combination with your offerings.

Idea in Brief

The Problem

Many companies that sell products or services either don't realize they could turn their offerings into a platform business or struggle to do so.

The Opportunity

By becoming a multisided platform (MSP) that facilitates interactions between parties, a company may be able to provide new revenue sources while also preventing competitors from stealing market share from its product or service.

The Solution

Here are four scenarios whereby regular products or services can become MSPs. The authors take into account the advantages and pitfalls of each and the resources, relationships, and organizational changes that would be required.

Consider three examples:

Intuit is the leading seller of financial management, accounting, and tax software products for consumers and small businesses in the United States. In the past six years or so it has taken significant steps to turn QuickBooks, its flagship financial-accounting product for small businesses, into an MSP. It opened up application-programming interfaces and introduced a developer program and an app store to allow third-party developers to build and sell software products to QuickBooks' customer base. Those products leverage data about small-business finances provided by QuickBooks. Since 2013 QuickBooks has also enabled its customers to apply directly to several third-party financial institutions for loans through a service called QuickBooks Financing.

Health clubs are increasingly renting space inside their gyms to specialty studios so that the latter can serve health club members. This allows a club to offer a greater variety of classes, which helps it retain existing members and attract new ones. For instance, the Forum Athletic Club, in Atlanta, recently reached an agreement with Cyc Fitness, a national cycling-studio chain, which now operates a self-contained studio inside the Forum's 22,000-square-foot gym.

The Lawson chain of convenience stores in Japan started in the 1990s to turn its shops into MSPs that facilitate transactions between its customers and third-party service providers. Today Lawson customers can pay utility bills and insurance premiums, ship and pick up parcels through postal service providers, and claim items ordered from e-commerce sites just by visiting their local convenience store.

For your product or service to become a true MSP in this scenario, at least some of the connection between your customers and third parties must be made through your product. Intuit could simply have sold aggregated (and anonymized) QuickBooks data to third-party developers and financial institutions. That would have added a potentially profitable new offering for Intuit, but it would not have turned QuickBooks into an MSP that could exploit network effects.

For this type of transition to make sense, your product or service must have an established brand and a large customer base—but that alone won't elicit interest from third parties. It must also meet one or both of the following conditions:

It serves a baseline need for many customers, yet leaves a large number of heterogeneous customer needs unserved. You can encourage and enable third parties to fill those gaps with products and services that are typically complementary to yours. Most third-party apps in Intuit's app store target market niches and customer needs not served by QuickBooks on its own.

It generates frequent customer interactions. That makes it a good candidate to become a one-stop shop for other, not necessarily complementary products and services. The third-party services that Lawson's customers can access are largely unrelated to its own products and services, but customers find it extremely convenient to access all of them in the same location.

It's important to be aware of several pitfalls associated with this approach to an MSP. One is that customers who come to you primarily for a product or service may object to the advertising of third-party offerings, especially if they are paying for yours. Intuit faced this when it started exploring services to offer through QuickBooks. As a result, the company is very careful to allow only offerings that align well with the needs and desires of QuickBooks customers and to obtain explicit consent to participate in tests for targeted third-party offers. In addition, Intuit has rebranded QuickBooks as "the operating system for small business" precisely to change customers' perceptions and to minimize potential backlash.

Another possible pitfall is that because you have an existing provider relationship with your customers, they may hold you responsible for the quality of their interactions with third parties. By enabling those parties to interact with your customers, you are implicitly endorsing their offerings—to a greater extent than does a company born as a multisided platform. For instance, a customer taking a spinning class offered by a third-party studio in a health club's gym is likely to blame the health club for a bad experience. As a result, you must curate third-party products and services much more carefully than a company born as an MSP has to.

Finally, some third-party products and services may cannibalize your offerings. The natural inclination would be to allow only those that are either complementary or unrelated to yours. But that approach can be misguided. In some cases it may make sense to coopt offerings that compete somewhat with yours and capture some of the resulting value to your customers. The Forum Athletic Club has replaced its own cycling classes with the Cyc Fitness classes offered at its gym. Cyc's spinning classes have proved more popular with members and allow the Forum to focus its resources on other services while converting Cyc from a competitor to a complementor.

The underlying logic is that if substitution from third parties is inevitable, bringing them onto your platform may expand its overall appeal to your customers, resulting in more demand and opportunities to sell your own services. It may also encourage you to reevaluate your offering's core competitive advantages and focus on them, which may mean ceding ground to third parties in some areas.

2. Connecting Customers

In this scenario you are selling a product or service to two distinct customer segments that interact or transact with each other outside your offering. You can become an MSP by modifying or expanding your offering so that at least some element of those interactions or transactions occurs through your product or service.

Quickbooks is used by both small businesses and accounting professionals. Intuit is in the process of adding a matchmaking function within QuickBooks that would enable small businesses to find and contact accountants with relevant expertise in their geographic area and would allow already-matched business-accountant pairs to exchange documents through the product.

Garmin and other fitness wearables are used by both consumers and personal trainers. Many companies that offer these products also host online systems (Garmin Connect, for example) to store fitness-training and health data. Garmin could enable users to share their data with personal trainers, thereby enhancing the interactions between those two groups. To further capture value from this strategy, Garmin could charge trainers for a "pro" subscription—software tools that would let them access clients' data to oversee activities and progress.

This scenario highlights how different customer segments of the same product or service can become customer groups on an MSP. For example, men and women are customer segments for a hair salon (no interaction between them is facilitated by the salon), but they are customer groups for a heterosexual dating service. An entrepreneurial hair salon that started offering matchmaking services to its customer segments could convert men and women into customer groups.

There are two pitfalls associated with this strategy. First, you run the risk of wasting resources on a feature that ultimately creates little additional value for your customers or your company. Worse, the MSP feature can be a detriment if customers perceive it as misaligned with the value of your underlying product or service. Some customers of a hair salon that provides matchmaking services might not want to risk encountering matches that didn't work out. Others might worry that offering a dating service means the salon isn't focused on giving the highest-quality haircuts.

Blizzard Entertainment's ill-fated Auction House for its popular Diablo video game provides a cautionary tale. Having noticed that Diablo players were routinely trading digital items on eBay and other external platforms, Blizzard created the Auction House in 2012 to make those transactions easier. It allowed players to buy and sell digital items in exchange for "gold" (digital currency in the Diablo game) as well as real dollars—and Blizzard was able to charge a transaction fee. It quickly became clear, however, that this feature created perverse incentives. Many players decided that buying items at the Auction House was an easier way to reach the game's advanced stages than devoting several hours to killing monsters and searching for loot inside the game. Other players strove to accumulate game items for the sole purpose of selling them in the Auction House. Realizing that this behavior was undermining the value of the game itself, Blizzard shut down the Auction House in 2014.

It is imperative that you conduct market research or run experiments to answer the following questions: Would significant proportions of our offering's various customer segments derive substantial benefits from interacting or transacting with one another? If yes, can our product or service enhance those interactions in a significant way? How will our customers react to the addition of an MSP feature, and how will that feature affect the way they interact with the original offering?

The second pitfall, as in scenario number one, is that although your offering is now simply facilitating a connection or a transaction between two parties, if one party is dissatisfied with the other, you may be held partly responsible. That means you need to put governance mechanisms in place to minimize (if not eliminate) the likelihood of unsatisfactory interactions. Intuit will have to carefully curate the accountants it recommends to QuickBooks customers through its matchmaking feature.

3. Connecting Products to Connect Customers

In this scenario you are selling two products or services, each to a different customer base, and the two customer bases interact outside your offerings. You can become an MSP by modifying or expanding your offerings so that at least part of those interactions occurs through one or both of your offerings.

Cards Against Humanity is a popular game in which players complete fill-in-the-blank statements with humorous (and often tasteless) words or phrases printed on physical playing cards. Its creators continue to sell the game and its numerous expansion packs to consumers, but they have also created Blackbox, a separate website through which they sell back-end fulfillment services (credit-card processing, customer service, shipping) to independent artists who want to sell their products—including third-party developers of other card games. Currently these are separate offerings, but the company could create an MSP by linking them. For instance, it could allow Blackbox customers to advertise their games to Cards Against Humanity's users with expansion packs. A more sophisticated implementation would allow Blackbox customers to test game concepts on willing Cards Against Humanity users, who would provide feedback.

Credit bureaus such as Equifax, Experian, and TransUnion offer a suite of services for consumers (access to credit scores, identity theft protection, and so on) and a suite of services for financial institutions (credit reports on consumers and businesses). These suites are based on the same data, but the two types of customers interact outside the services (as when a consumer applies for a mortgage); the credit bureaus do not directly facilitate those interactions.

Credit bureaus could create online MSPs where consumers could obtain their credit scores and receive targeted offers from financial institutions. (This is the business model of start-ups such as Credit Karma and Lendio.) These MSPs could go further and enable consumers to create and manage a digital data profile that they could then use to apply directly for financial products at participating institutions (similar to the way Intuit allows QuickBooks customers to apply for financial products through QuickBooks Financing).

Nielsen offers "watch" products to media companies (data on consumers' viewing habits) and "buy" products to consumer goods manufacturers (data on consumers' purchasing habits). One could easily imagine Nielsen's adding the ability for a consumer-packaged-goods company to connect with relevant media companies for advertising purposes.

This scenario highlights how a multiproduct company can become a multisided platform that benefits from network effects. For example, by increasing sales of credit and identity-theft-protection products to consumers, credit bureaus can improve their offerings for financial institutions (which leverage consumer data), thereby achieving greater cross-product economies of scope. While that alone might be valuable, credit bureaus could create and capture even more value by linking the two kinds of products to facilitate interactions between consumers and financial institutions (as described above). This would create an MSP and generate network effects: If more consumers use the credit and identity-theft-protection products, that increases the value of the offerings for financial institutions, which can then transact with more consumers more effectively and vice versa.

Two risks are associated with this strategy. First, as with scenario number two, you may waste resources on a feature that ultimately creates little value for your customers or your company relative to the underlying product or service. Second, optimizing for interactions between customers of different products may lead to design choices that limit the growth potential of one or the other product on its own. Once again, it is imperative to use market research and experiments to answer a few questions: Would considerable proportions of your offerings' respective customers derive significantly greater benefits from interacting or transacting through you? If yes, can your offerings substantially enhance those interactions? How will the customers of your two offerings react to the addition of an MSP feature? How will that feature affect the way customers interact with the original products?

4. Supplying to a Multisided Platform

In this scenario you become an MSP by creating an offering for your customers' customers that enhances the value of the product or service they buy from your customers. (Although this strategy is logically possible, we are not yet aware of examples of its successful implementation.)

It is important to emphasize that this strategy goes beyond the more traditional "ingredient brand" strategy, which is also a "customers' customers" approach. Indeed, some (essential) ingredient suppliers have created brands in the eyes of their customers' customers (for example, Intel's "Intel Inside") that allow them to extract more value from their customers. But because these ingredient suppliers offer no products or services directly to their customers' customers, they are not MSPs.

The major pitfall with this scenario is that your customers are likely to react negatively to any attempt to go after their customers. Nevertheless, we believe this strategy could work under certain circumstances. The key is to convince your customers that the product or service you provide to their customers is truly complementary to—rather than competitive with—their own offerings.

Shopify is a leading provider of e-commerce tools to online and retail merchants. Currently the company has no direct connection with its customers' users. It could, however, start offering a common log-in or loyalty program to users of its customers' sites. Whether such an initiative would be successful would hinge on whether Shopify could persuade its merchant customers that the offering was a valuable added service rather than simply an attempt to take control of their customer relationships.

The decision whether and how to convert an offering into an MSP should be informed by who your current customers are, how you currently interact with them, and how they interact with one another. The most fundamental challenge associated with this endeavor is transitioning from a world in which you have 100% control over what your customers are offered to one in which you can only influence the value that is created for them (by third parties or by interactions among themselves).

A final consideration is organizational and leadership challenges. If a company has a solid reputation that is rooted in creating and offering products, shifting to an MSP-focused strategy might be difficult for employees who deeply identify with those products. And companies that sell successful products or services often have strong research and development operations and many engineers in leadership roles; shifting to an MSP strategy that depends on the adept management of third-party relationships might require putting business-development and marketing professionals in significant leadership roles, generating internal conflict. Furthermore, as a company's strategy moves from a product or service orientation to being more MSP-centric, boards, CEOs, and senior management teams may find it difficult to deal with multiple or hybrid strategies, adopt and track new performance metrics, and enforce some degree of technological or customer experience consistency between previously separate products and services.

Nevertheless, if you decide that creating a platform will provide great opportunities for growth and increased profitability and thwart potential competitive threats, the effort to make the transformation may well be worthwhile.

Originally published in July–August 2017. Reprint R1704G

What's Your Google Strategy?

by Andrei Hagiu and David B. Yoffie

WHEN TOYS "R" US EXECUTIVES SIGNED a 10-year "exclusive" agreement with Amazon in 2000, they saw the deal as the perfect solution to a vexing challenge: how to establish an online retail business that would dominate its category and achieve profitability sooner rather than later. Having struggled to build an online business on their own, they believed they needed Amazon's internet savvy and order-fulfillment skills. They agreed to pay Amazon a hefty $50 million annually plus a percentage of the toy retailer's online sales in exchange for Amazon's building and running a Toys "R" Us virtual storefront on its e-commerce site. Less than four years later, the deal had turned into a money loser for Toys "R" Us, and the company sued Amazon, seeking $200 million in damages.

What went wrong? To fuel its own growth and profitability, Amazon had recruited small, third-party merchants to sell toys and games directly through its website. In a two-year court battle, Toys "R" Us argued that Amazon had violated the exclusivity agreement and that the rising competition had hurt its online sales. Amazon tried to justify its actions by contending that the other merchants were addressing customer needs that Toys "R" Us couldn't or wouldn't satisfy. In the end, the court ruled that Amazon had violated the agreement; it allowed the companies to sever their relationship but didn't award Toys "R" Us damages.

Toys "R" Us's frustration is not unique. Companies large and small have been wandering in the wilderness, trying to figure out how to play with the rapidly growing number of multisided platforms such as Amazon. MSPs are products, services, or technologies that connect different types of customers to one another. Credit-card companies and eBay link consumers and merchants. Google's search engine connects advertisers and users of its services. Microsoft's Windows platform has three sides (application developers, users, and OEMs), as does the Blu-ray standard for high-definition DVDs (content providers, manufacturers of DVD players, and consumers). Once a relatively obscure strategic problem, multisided platforms have become important for all companies today, thanks to the power of the internet and related technologies. As new intermediaries have emerged to facilitate search capabilities and reduce transaction costs, companies find themselves acting either as an MSP or as a player on someone else's MSP.

MSPs are doubled-edged swords for the average company. On the one hand, a platform can make a company more efficient or increase its customer reach. For example, by advertising on Google, a firm can gain access to an audience that otherwise may be impossibly expensive to attract. On the other hand, just because an MSP has a great installed base of customers or offers platform services that can significantly reduce costs does not mean that joining it guarantees success. Before Toys "R" Us struck its deal with Amazon, it should have recognized that the two companies' long-term interests were fundamentally at odds. The success of Amazon's platform depended on covering the "long tail" of consumer demand by offering any product in any category. By contrast, Toys "R" Us's success was driven by the "short tail" of toys: pushing mainly hot products in high demand. Toys "R" Us should have anticipated that as soon as it succeeded in establishing the toys and games category on Amazon's platform, Amazon would have the upper hand and would try to wiggle out of the exclusivity pact. Toys "R" Us probably should not have agreed to put its online store inside Amazon's site. At the very least, it should have extracted more concessions (including tougher restrictions on adding other toy vendors) up front, when its power was the greatest.

Idea in Brief

Multisided platforms (think intermediaries like Amazon or eBay that connect interdependent groups of customers) can lower your transaction costs and increase customer reach. But, as Toys "R" Us learned when it teamed up with Amazon, choosing the wrong MSP can lead to stiffer competition and loss of control over customers.

To select the right MSP for your business, consider three crucial decisions:

- Should you use an existing MSP or build your own platform?

- Should your company partner with one MSP or many? For instance, many companies advertise on both Google and Yahoo!

- Which MSP features should you adopt—or reject—to maintain competitive advantage? Target preserved its brand by selectively using Amazon's order-fulfillment services on its own website.

Without a clear strategy for dealing with multisided platforms, firms can easily find themselves ceding control over customers or being unwittingly turned into commodities. A few basic steps can help managers set a clear platform strategy:

- First, decide whether to play with an existing MSP, build your own platform, or do both.

- If you conclude that a third-party MSP can benefit your business, determine whether your company should join one or many.

- Once you know which MSPs to play with, figure out how to play—which features or services you should adopt and which you should reject in order to maintain your competitive advantage.

To Play or Not to Play?

It might seem obvious that all companies should play with platforms that can add value to their business. Indeed, in some industries

Idea in Practice

A closer look at the three decisions:

Use an Existing MSP—Or Build Your Own?

An existing MSP may use its power against you to capture more value for itself. Watch out for these moves:

- **Imposing price increases once the MSP becomes successful.** After the PC market tipped to Windows, Microsoft raised its license price to OEMs.

- **Vertically integrating into players' businesses.** Google has been bundling more applications into its core offerings.

- **Weakening your relationship with your customers.** Retailing giants that joined Amazon had

difficulty differentiating themselves from smaller merchants piling onto the site.

Given these risks, you may want to build an MSP (proprietary or open) yourself or with other players. That's expensive. Do so only if:

- You're a strategic player: You wield substantial power in the market relative to established MSPs and other players—so you can influence the MSP's actions.

- You can team up with enough other players to create a new MSP.

Partner with One MSP—Or Many?

- With MSPs that don't require exclusivity: Consider joining all those that offer you positive net

there is no choice: If you want to write applications for PCs or games, you have to work on MSPs such as Windows, Macintosh, or PlayStation. Your initial bias should be to join an MSP for two reasons: the immediate opportunity to reduce search and transaction costs and the expense and risk of building your own. But before leaping onto an MSP, you should carefully consider one major risk: the potential for the company (or companies) that owns or controls an MSP to hold you up—to use its power against you to capture more value for itself.

The most obvious form of holdup is the price increases that companies can and often do impose once their MSPs become successful. After the PC market tipped to Windows, Microsoft raised the price of its license to OEMs almost every other year for two decades. A company can also hold up players by using the MSP to vertically value. For example, advertise on Google *and* Yahoo!

- If an MSP demands exclusivity: That can present an opportunity. An MSP that needs you may offer money in exchange for an exclusive relationship.

Example: Satellite radio provider Sirius paid $500 million for an exclusive contract with radio personality Howard Stern to gain the upper hand over its rival XM.

Adopt Which MSP Features?

Use MSPs in ways that will enable you to:

- Differentiate yourself from competitors conducting business on the same platform

- Reduce the risk of an MSP using its power against you

Example: When Google launched a social networking application development platform, OpenSocial, it invited other social networking sites to use OpenSocial applications. Social networking site LinkedIn joined in, but to preserve its distinctiveness compared with other networking sites, it has been selective about which OpenSocial applications it will allow to work with LinkedIn. In addition, LinkedIn continues to offer unique applications; for instance, an events calendar that allows a LinkedIn member to find which members from LinkedIn and other networks are attending events.

integrate into their businesses. The more successful a player is, the greater the temptation is for the MSP to try to capture that value for itself. And the MSP has considerable power to do so: The company that controls a successful MSP controls the interface between players and end users and dictates the rules of engagement. This form of holdup has become pervasive in technology-based industries where the dividing line between players and platforms is easily crossed. Microsoft's practice of invading other companies' turf by adding features to Office and Explorer is well known, but it's hardly the only example: eBay expanded into payment systems; Google has been bundling more and more applications into its core offerings; and Facebook has been introducing features previously provided by its third-party vendors.

Platforms, Market Intermediaries, and Multisided Platforms

Pure Platforms

Platforms are products, services, or technologies that serve as foundations on which other parties can build complementary products, services, or technologies. Pure platforms do not have any contact with players' customers.

Examples: SAP's ERP software, E-Ink's electronic ink technology (used in the Amazon Kindle), Qualcomm's CDMA technology for mobile devices

Pure Market Intermediaries

Market intermediaries are firms that make a living by reducing search and transactions costs for two or more distinct groups of players. These firms generally take full possession or control of the goods and services whose sale they facilitate.

Examples: Walmart, 7-Eleven, Whole Foods

Multisided Platforms

An MSP is both a platform and an intermediary. MSPs can insert themselves between you and your customers, though they don't take ownership of the goods and services whose sale they facilitate. MSPs support players that are interdependent, which creates indirect network effects.

Examples: Nintendo Wii, Amazon.com, Match.com

The third way an MSP can hold you up is by using its power to weaken your relationship with your customers—either by gradually taking control over end customers or by inviting other players to compete in your product category. Obviously, this can greatly reduce a player's ability to extract value. Aside from Toys "R" Us, several other retailers, including Borders, Circuit City, Gap, and HMV, rushed to join the Amazon platform between 2000 and 2001, only to realize a few years later that they were having a hard time differentiating their offerings from the increasing numbers of smaller merchants piling onto the site. Eventually, all these big retailers dropped Amazon and went with their own web platforms. But by that time, they had lost valuable years.

Some companies claim that they will never use their MSPs to compete with their players, but you should not take such commitments at face value. The president of one multibillion-dollar online retailer we interviewed had the right attitude. He told us that even though a platform's initial sales pitch may sound great, "I assume they want to screw us. For example, PayPal and Google want us to take their payment system, but for us, they are a Trojan horse." In the face of holdup threats, you should seriously consider building a platform on your own or with other players. If you wield substantial power in the market or can team up with enough other players to gain the upper hand, building a platform yourself or with others may be the way to go. The test of whether you have enough power is: Can you influence the MSP's actions? Those companies that can we call "strategic players."

Strategic players can choose from two broad do-it-yourself approaches. The first is to build a proprietary platform (by yourself or with partners) in order to create value and capture as much of it as possible. The second do-it-yourself approach is to create an open MSP, which prevents any platform from ever claiming value. Google's Android operating system (for mobile phones) and OpenSocial application programming interface (for developing applications for social networks) can be viewed as an attempt to do just that. The search giant wants to prevent Symbian, Microsoft, or Apple from becoming the dominant operating system for mobile devices, and it wants to prevent Facebook and MySpace from dominating social networks.

Companies make two common mistakes in deciding whether or not to play with an existing MSP. First, they fail to fully understand the objectives of the MSP's owner and how those objectives might change over time as the MSP's growing power creates opportunities to extract more value from its players. For instance, providing technology or order-fulfillment services to third-party sellers makes up only 5% of Amazon's revenues but accounts for a full 30% of the company's profits. Some retailers recognized the benefits and dangers of the Amazon platform and played their cards well. Target, for example, decided not to create a storefront within Amazon.com and instead built a 100% Target-branded website that used some of Amazon's order-fulfillment services.

The second common mistake in deciding whether to build their own proprietary platform is that some companies grossly overestimate their own ability to persuade other players to support it. Nokia fell into this trap.

After introducing smartphones in 1996, Nokia realized that it needed a software platform that would encourage the development of sophisticated applications and mobile services. Rather than rely on Palm OS or Microsoft's Windows Mobile, the leading software platforms for handheld devices at the time, Nokia persuaded three other handset manufacturers to join it in creating Symbian, a for-profit consortium that would develop a new operating system. Initially, Nokia held the largest stake, around 40%.

Symbian licensed its operating system to its shareholders as well as to any other mobile phone manufacturer that wanted it, and it quickly became the leading smartphone operating system, with a market share of more than 60%. But to differentiate themselves in the fiercely competitive market, licensees then developed customized, incompatible versions of the operating system. The resulting fragmentation prevented the platform from becoming popular with application developers. After more than seven years on the market, only about 5,000 applications had been built. (More than 10,000 applications were built for Apple's iPhone OS in less than a year.)

In addition, Nokia's leading stake in the venture caused other handset manufacturers to fear that Nokia would use its power to gain an advantage over them. They hedged their bets by supporting various versions of Linux and Windows Mobile as well as Symbian. That left a huge opening for existing competitors to catch up and for newcomers such as Google's Android and Apple's iPhone to enter the fray.

In a last-ditch effort to save the Symbian operating system, Nokia bought out its partners and spun off the enterprise in June 2008 as an open source consortium that gave its software away. In

To Play or Not to Play?

QUESTIONS TO ASK when deciding whether to play

- What parts of our business are we doing ourselves that would be better handled by using an existing multisided platform?
- What are the things that we rely on MSPs for that we should be doing ourselves?
- Can existing MSPs add value to our business by lowering our costs or increasing our customer reach at a reasonable price?
- What are the risks that an MSP will use its power against us to capture more value for itself?
- What conditions might allow the MSP to raise prices over time?
- Is there a danger that the MSP will try to take control of our customers and reduce our differentiation?
- Should we pursue a "do it yourself" (DIY) strategy and build our own platform?
- What are the feasible DIY options (by ourselves or in a coalition with other players)?
- Would we pursue a DIY strategy to claim value for ourselves or to prevent other MSPs from claiming value?
- If we build a platform, will other players join us? Can we achieve sufficient scale without working through an established MSP?

essence, Nokia recognized that it had erred in trying to use a proprietary platform to contain or deter competing platforms while also attempting to extract value for itself. But it may have learned this too late. Companies rarely get a second chance to tip a market.

Which MSP Should We Play With?

If you decide that you should play with one or more MSPs, then you have to figure out which to join. More specifically, should you go with one MSP exclusively or affiliate with several?

Some MSPs may not require exclusivity, in which case you should consider joining all those that offer positive net value. For example, since neither Google nor Yahoo requires exclusive arrangements, there's no reason not to advertise on both.

Other MSPs may demand exclusivity, which can be an opportunity. If an MSP wants and needs you, it may offer money or other forms of compensation in exchange for an exclusive relationship. The most visible example in recent times was the battle between the Toshiba-led HD DVD camp and the Sony-led Blu-ray camp to be the dominant platform for high-definition DVDs. Both sides reportedly offered large sums to Paramount, DreamWorks, Disney, and other studios to persuade them to join on an exclusive basis.

Similarly, hot content producers have been able to rake in enormous sums by getting rival radio and TV broadcasters to bid against each other for exclusive access to their content. Satellite radio provider Sirius paid $500 million for a five-year exclusive contract with radio personality Howard Stern to gain the upper hand over its rival XM.

In the long run, perhaps the most critical considerations for strategic players are: Would an exclusive relationship with you tip the market to one platform or another? If so, do you want to tip the market and allow one winner to take all? Tipping is desirable when adopting one standard would expand the market for all players and it's still possible to prevent the MSP from holding you up. Otherwise, a strategic player should steer clear of the arrangement and maintain support for two or more competing MSPs. Samsung and Motorola adroitly adopted this approach in mobile phones and played with multiple MSPs: Symbian, Windows Mobile, Linux, and Palm OS. This strategy made sense for them because it was (and still is) very hard to tell which platform might win, and neither was large enough to tip the market to one operating system. The downside of this hedging strategy, of course, is obviously the extra engineering, marketing, and support required to play with several MSPs.

Indecisiveness in choosing where to play can be expensive. Time Warner arguably made this mistake in the high-definition DVD standards war. For more than two years, Time Warner supported both HD DVD and Blu-ray. It initially hoped that HD DVD would win for a number of reasons: Time Warner had a higher market share for content on HD DVD than it did on Blu-ray (50% versus 20%); HD DVD players were cheaper, which meant that the market for machines and content would grow faster if that standard prevailed; and the company was reluctant to throw its weight behind a platform led by Sony, one of its main competitors. But with the overall market evenly split between the two standards, Time Warner was unwilling to gamble and exclusively back HD DVD—especially since Sony, which had lost the VHS-Betamax wars in the 1980s and had bet its PlayStation 3 franchise on Blu-ray, could be expected to fight until the bloody end.

Eventually, Time Warner's fears about helping Sony were supplanted by the concern that the long-term opportunity to sell high-definition DVDs was shrinking. One factor was that the continuing uncertainty about which standard would prevail was slowing consumer purchases of high-definition players. The second was that digital downloads were rapidly eating into the market for DVDs. Time Warner couldn't do much about the second factor, but it could do something about the first by helping tip the market to one standard. Realizing that its 50% share of HD DVD content gave it more power over HD DVD's fate than its 20% share of Blu-ray content gave it over Blu-ray's, Time Warner decided in early 2008 to abandon the HD DVD camp, which immediately called it quits.

But Time Warner's indecision clearly hurt its long-term profits. It would have been better off making an exclusive commitment earlier—in exchange for a sufficiently large payment to compensate for the risk of guessing wrong about who the ultimate winner would be. Given all the previous occasions when delays in resolving standards wars had opened the gate for new technologies to leapfrog existing ones, Time Warner should have known better.

How to Play

In choosing how to play on a given platform, companies must keep two main questions in mind: How can we differentiate ourselves from competitors that are conducting business on the same platform? And how can we reduce or mitigate the risk of holdup once we have decided to play?

Where to Play?

QUESTIONS TO ASK when deciding where to play:

- Does the multisided platform require exclusivity, or can we play on multiple MSPs?

- How does the increase in customer reach from playing on multiple MSPs compare with the increase in costs from supporting multiple MSPs?

- Can we extract extra compensation from an MSP if we go exclusive? Does the extra compensation outweigh the loss of customer reach and flexibility from playing with multiple MSPs?

- Would we tip the market to one MSP by going exclusive?

- Do we want or need to tip the market, or do we want to prevent it from tipping?

- What are the benefits and costs associated with the market tipping?

- What are the benefits and costs associated with the market not tipping?

For nonstrategic players that lack the power to influence an MSP's actions, deciding how to play usually boils down to choosing from the menu of contracts offered by an MSP. For example, after a company has decided to place online ads through Google, the only remaining choices are how much to spend and which keywords to bid on. But in some cases, even a nonstrategic player can make choices that will differentiate it from competitors and avoid contract options that could commoditize its business. LinkedIn clearly kept those issues in mind when deciding how to play on Google's OpenSocial platform.

When Google announced in 2007 that it was going to launch OpenSocial, a new platform for developing applications that would work on all social network websites that joined it, LinkedIn had to decide whether it should play with Google and, if so, how. The decision to play was relatively easy. LinkedIn, as the third-largest social network behind MySpace and Facebook, needed to extend its reach and potentially lower its costs in order to compete. The critical question was, how to play?

Google's motive for launching OpenSocial was clear: to commoditize the leaders, increase competition among social networks in

How to Play?

QUESTIONS TO ASK when deciding how to play:

- Which services or features of the multisided platform will enhance our differentiation and which will commoditize our business?

- How do the MSP's terms affect our competitive advantage relative to other players on the MSP?

- Do the terms strengthen the MSP's ability to hold us up?

- Should we (and do we have to) choose from the menu of contracts offered by the MSP? Can we negotiate a custom offering to mitigate the risk of holdup or commoditization?

general, and make it easier for Google to sell advertising. If "gated" communities such as Facebook or MySpace were more open to everyone on the web, there might be huge opportunities to sell advertising.

Recognizing these dangers, LinkedIn crafted a strategy that would exploit the advantages of the platform but mitigate most of the risks. It decided to build its own platform and invite third-party application developers to join. In addition, it decided it would not allow all applications developed for OpenSocial members to work on LinkedIn. It would continue to offer proprietary applications and would use OpenSocial to increase their value. For example, it added to its proprietary calendar application an OpenSocial feature that allows a LinkedIn member to find out who else from LinkedIn and other networks is attending an event. Though it was a nonstrategic player in the space, LinkedIn consciously took steps to avoid becoming trapped in a commodity world, by mixing and matching the advantages of the MSP with its own products.

Strategic players have more options. They can either order from the menu or use their power to obtain a custom deal. A good example is the way Electronic Arts, the world's largest video-game developer and publisher, forced Microsoft's Xbox division to accede to its demands in online gaming.

Microsoft had required that game companies use its proprietary tools in developing their online games, include standardized features such as voice chat and Gamertags (unique user names), and allow Microsoft to handle customer service, billing, and administration. EA feared that those terms would cede too much control of the user relationship to Microsoft and would level the playing field among game developers. It also worried that it would set a bad precedent, encouraging Microsoft to make even more onerous demands in the future. Moreover, EA felt that Microsoft's refusal to share Xbox Live subscription fees with game publishers was unfair. Consequently, it refused to go along. To put pressure on Microsoft, EA included online functionality in the versions of the games it made for the Sony PlayStation 2, but not for the Xbox versions. Recognizing that this put Xbox Live at a severe disadvantage, Microsoft caved. It allowed EA to maintain control over its own user data, marketing, and billing and reportedly also agreed to give EA financial compensation.

The biggest mistake you can make when deciding how to play is granting preferential terms to an MSP without carefully analyzing how the terms will affect the balance of power, both now and in the future. Failing to keep options open when you don't want the market to tip can put you at a significant disadvantage if the market does tip. This has been a painful lesson for the music studios in their relationship with Apple and iTunes. To contain the mortal threat posed by Napster and other file-sharing services, the studios hastily jumped on the iTunes platform in 2001. As a result, iTunes became the dominant platform for digital music, the studios found themselves dependent on it, and Apple has been able to extract most of the value of the business—mainly by keeping all the proceeds of its highly profitable iPod sales for itself. The studios should have considered the long-term implications of their decision to join iTunes more carefully and tried to negotiate more advantageous terms from the outset.

Playing with multisided platforms soon will be a fact of life for all companies, big and small. MSPs reduce search and transaction costs and give companies vastly broader access to markets than they could achieve on their own. But over the past 10 years, we've also seen powerful owners of MSPs like Microsoft, Google, and Apple extract most of the value from platforms, because companies that played with them didn't adequately understand their motives and operating strategies.

So resist the herd mentality. Think twice before you join a popular platform. And remember that MSPs are moving targets and regularly review your strategy. The Google of tomorrow is unlikely to be the same platform as the Google of today. What's more, today's player can become tomorrow's platform. Until the iPhone was invented, most cell phone companies were players on the platforms of cellular networks. In the last two years, first the iPhone and then a slew of other cell phone manufacturers have rushed to turn themselves into the next-generation platform. Players should be on the lookout for opportunities to become the tail that wags the dog. If you play really well on an MSP, you may even be able to dictate the rules of the game.

Originally published in April 2009. Reprint R0904F

In the Ecosystem Economy, What's Your Strategy?

by Michael G. Jacobides

WHEN NESTLÉ WAS PREPARING to go mainstream with Nespresso, its single-use espresso capsule, it knew that users would need a machine specifically designed to work with the pod. So the company cultivated a network of manufacturers. It didn't tell customers to buy a Jura, a Krups, or a Braun—it just decided which manufacturers could be on the list. And because the capsule and its interface were patented, other manufacturers could not make Nespresso-compatible machines without permission.

Nespresso was creating—designing—an ecosystem: an orchestrated network spanning multiple sectors. The firms involved work to shared standards, sometimes on a shared platform, to make their products and services compatible. And they create links among themselves that make it difficult for outsiders to break in.

Designed ecosystems like Nespresso's are increasingly important, owing to the convergence of three big structural changes in our economy. The first is an unprecedented rollback of regulations protecting firms that once had the exclusive privilege of serving particular customer needs. As those protections fall, organizations in other domains are free to partner to provide more-integrated offerings, as when accountancies team up with law firms. The second change is a blurring of the separation between products and services because of regulatory changes and digitization. The latter has also led to offerings with more-modular structures whose components can be recombined in new ways, which in turn has encouraged the rise of product-service bundles provided by networks of interdependent suppliers. The third change involves technology that is revolutionizing how firms can serve their customers. Our dependence on mobile devices, along with the internet's influence on buying patterns, has dramatically expanded the possibilities for linking previously unrelated goods and services—reinforcing the effects of the first two changes.

Given these shifts, it is less and less likely that single firms can offer all the elements a customer needs—let alone afford to experiment with them. And so ecosystems, especially designed ones, are on the rise. In fact, in a growing number of sectors the firm and even the industry have ceased to be meaningful units of strategic analysis. We must focus instead on competition between digitally enabled designed ecosystems that span traditional industry boundaries and offer complex and customizable product-service bundles.

Traditional strategy frameworks are of little help when designing or participating in such an ecosystem. An ecosystem-focused framework, as opposed to a firm-focused one, needs to answer five questions.

1. Can You Help Other Firms Create Value?

In ecosystem competition, success is as much about helping other firms innovate as it is about being innovative yourself. Companies that have built a successful ecosystem have often done so incrementally, broadening the value proposition of their core offering by finding opportunities to apply one of its features or functionalities to some previously unrelated product or service.

Consider Google's Nest, which started by developing a smart digital thermostat that can be controlled remotely. It then added an alarm, thus building a bundle that controls both comfort and security. Next, capitalizing on the possibilities of digital interconnections, it

Idea in Brief

The Challenge

In an increasing number of contexts, the firm is no longer an independent strategic actor. Its success depends on collaboration with other firms in an ecosystem spanning multiple sectors.

Why It Arose

The growing importance of ecosystems is linked to the convergence of three big structural changes: a rollback of regulatory protections, a blurring of the separation between products and services, and technology that revolutionizes how firms can serve customers.

How to Meet It

An ecosystem-focused framework can help managers answer five key questions: *Can you help other firms create value? What role should you play? What should the terms be? Can your organization adapt?* and *How many ecosystems should you manage?*

created the Works with Nest ecosystem, which lets firms innovate by connecting with Nest. For instance, LIFX designed a Nest-compatible system whereby red LEDs flash if the smoke or safety alarms are activated—a literal lifesaver for the hard of hearing. Fitbit, the wearable fitness tracker, can tell Nest you're awake so that it knows to warm your home. And Mercedes-Benz cars can use GPS to tell Nest to switch on the heat as you arrive. These extensions constitute a value proposition greater than anything Nest could have provided on its own. (Google recently announced that it will be phasing out Works with Nest and transitioning to Works with Google Assistant—an even broader and stronger ecosystem.)

That proposition rests on shared functionality. Nest may have started as a remotely controllable thermostat, but its creators realized that consumers might want to remotely control multiple services and products in multiple contexts. That understanding pointed the way to possible complementors, and Nest gradually migrated to providing remote control for a range of home systems and appliances.

Having identified a critical and shareable functionality, an ecosystem builder needs to consider the incentives and motivations of potential complementors. How will joining your ecosystem look from their point of view? Will they be content to remain comple-mentors, or could they reasonably hope to compete with you? In Nest's case, what value proposition could it offer Mercedes—that is, how could participation improve the way Mercedes embeds itself in its customers' daily lives? How did that compare with other options Mercedes had?

If you don't focus on the needs of your partners, your ecosys-tem will wither on the vine, no matter how strong your brand and market position; chances are that some other ecosystem builder can offer a better alternative. Nokia's downfall provides a cautionary example. Even though the firm's Symbian operating system started out as the de facto ruler of the mobile telephony space, it was soon eclipsed because Nokia focused on its own narrow needs. Treated as dispensable supply-chain subordinates, app developers and other complementors jumped ship to Android.

2. What Role Should You Play?

Many firms assume they should be the focus and chief architect of any ecosystem they create. That's not necessarily the case; some-times you are better off sharing the role or being a complementor.

To be the orchestrator and prime mover of an ecosystem, you need a superior product or service that is hard to replicate. This means some combination of IP protection, a large network of users, and strong branding. Nespresso, as mentioned, patented its capsule. The apps powering Uber and Facebook are so user-friendly that those companies very quickly built large user networks. And Apple's patent protection and user base are bolstered by a strong brand and large scale, positioning the company to orchestrate pretty much any ecosystem in which it participates.

Organizational and cultural factors are also critical. Few would disagree that orchestrators need the agility to respond to new chal-lengers, the humility to understand customer needs, and the vision to inspire complementors. But to say that isn't necessarily to state the obvious; consider the impact a single-minded focus on share-holder value and cost control can have on a company's ability to demonstrate those qualities. Firms with that focus are often, and sometimes rightly, accused of favoring the capture of short-term profits over the creation of long-term value—and given the time needed to shape an ecosystem's parts into a successful whole, that orientation could compromise a firm's ability to be an effective orchestrator. A company whose identity is deeply rooted in its technology or management system might also struggle. For example, an obsession with control could get in the way of engaging with entrepreneurial scientists, while a preference for organic, internally generated growth could lead to clashes with complementors equally protective of their turf.

If you lack the qualifications to build an ecosystem but have an IP-protected product or service that could anchor one, your best bet most likely involves attracting the interest of a large company that could buy into or license your idea. If a small-scale HVAC installer had come up with a remotely controllable thermostat, it probably could not have attracted the ecosystem of complementors that Google did. But it could have approached Google with the idea and served as a complementor while benefiting from licensing revenue. For many medium-size firms, a key strategy is to embed in many ecosystems. LIFX, for instance, connects with customers through Amazon's Alexa, Google Home, and Apple HomeKit.

Even if you bring a great product or service to the party and have the organizational and cultural capabilities to attract complementors, it might make sense to orchestrate in partnership with another firm in order to reach critical mass. Daimler and BMW recently announced plans to jointly create a managed-mobility ecosystem combining car sharing, ride hailing, parking, and other services. Concerned about disruption from firms such as Uber and Lyft, the automakers decided to collaborate on high-end services anchored to their brands—their chief differentiator and element of value, which a wholesale migration to mobility-as-a-service (MaaS) might well erode.

A big company can also buy into an ecosystem, which can be particularly helpful if its contribution is interchangeable with other firms' offerings. Toyota recently invested $1.5 billion in the Southeast

Asian ride-hailing company Grab, reasoning that MaaS will drive demand for reliable low-cost cars. That partnership, the company hopes, will give Toyota not just a direct edge as a car supplier but also an understanding of car usage patterns that could confer an advantage over rivals such as Hyundai and Nissan.

Some notes of caution for mainstream firms: Even if you are large, you may be vulnerable to disruption from Google, Apple, or other tech giants, and participating in one of their ecosystems as a complementor may have significant advantages over trying to orchestrate your own—especially when it's hard to assess what combination of products and services will satisfy the final customer, or when the range of potential combinations is very broad. You should probably not be responsible for entrepreneurial and creative inputs; in the video game industry, for example, developers organize flexibly through video game engines to take their offerings to consumers. And even if you ultimately want to build your own ecosystem, participating in another one can help you gain experience, understand the needs of customers and complementors, and build the skills that orchestrating requires.

3. What Should the Terms for Participation Be?

Research on ecosystem governance is still in its early days. But governance failures are easy to identify. For instance, as described earlier, Symbian failed in part because Nokia neglected to take other parties' interests into account. Contrast that with Apple's record with app developers.

There are two key governance choices.

Access

Early in the process an ecosystem builder needs to decide whether the system should be *open, managed,* or *closed.* In an open ecosystem (such as Uber's drivers), complementors need only meet certain basic standards to participate. In a managed ecosystem (such as Apple's App Store), there are clear criteria for complementors and possibly some limits on their number, along with specific guidelines—on functionality and pricing, say. In a closed ecosystem (such as VW's connected cars and Philips's digital health), approval of complementors and rules of participation are tightly controlled.

In general, the more open the system, the easier it is to attract complementors and a wide range of products—but quality is more variable. The degree of openness should be determined in part by what matters most to the final customer. For a mobile app platform with a diverse customer base, for example, an open ecosystem—one offering lots of choice—might make sense. But if quality and safety concerns arise, barriers may be in order. Think of DiDi, China's largest ride-hailing company. Reeling from the 2018 murders of two passengers by drivers for its Hitch service, the firm chose to become more closed; it suspended Hitch and now rigorously vets prospective DiDi drivers.

Attachment

As you determine how accessible to make your ecosystem, you'll also need to consider how exclusively attached to it you want your complementors to be—how much they need to cospecialize with you. There will be trade-offs for all parties. If your mobile operating system forbids app developers from porting their programs to other platforms, the developers will certainly have a stake in your success. But the restriction might cause them not to join if they have opportunities elsewhere. Conversely, if you impose no barriers to redeploying an app, you'll find it far easier to recruit complementors, but they will have no particular attachment to your ecosystem.

The degree to which an orchestrator can lock in complementors generally depends on the attractiveness of that orchestrator and what alternatives are available. A hugely attractive orchestrator such as Apple, which can link an app developer to a large and loyal network, can probably require more attachment than a new entrant can. Compared with Apple, Android was easy to join; Google wanted it to gain traction before scaling up. Symbian ignored its developers' increasing alternatives and collapsed when those developers decamped to Apple and Google.

Their power and attractiveness, along with a lack of alternatives, have historically given tech giants such as Apple and Google relatively free rein to aggressively manage access and attachment to their ecosystems. But as technologies and attitudes change, less hierarchical ecosystems are growing more popular. WeWork's meteoric rise resulted from the fact that it not only provides shared office space but also builds communities: The WeWork app allows members to collaborate with and provide services to one another with little interference. Not-for-profits, too, are setting up nonhierarchical ecosystems; one example is the Ellen MacArthur Foundation's CE100 network, which supports firms that promote the so-called circular economy. Some smaller ventures have gone in a similar direction: The London-based platform upstart Common Objective matches up companies in the fashion industry without imposing its own "rules of the game."

More radically, the rapid growth of ledger technologies such as blockchain opens up new possibilities for creating sets of interconnected companies. The members of these ecosystems are linked not through a hub firm but through a distributed system—designed by one company, perhaps, but used by many. Consider Blanc Labs' Nekso, the biggest challenger to Uber in Mexico City. Instead of assembling a fleet of individual drivers who connect with customers through an app (the Uber model), it built an interface that allows taxi companies to band together in a network passengers can choose from, providing the same seamless experience Uber offers but through a decentralized ecosystem.

4. Can Your Organization Adapt?

An ecosystem's members must be able to quickly adapt, because the needs of the final customer, along with the desire and ability of complementors to collaborate, can shift dramatically.

Take Nike's FuelBand, an early fitness tracker that connected with other Nike products. After the arrival of Fitbit and other competing products, Nike discontinued production; the market could easily serve the need it had met, diminishing the value-add of a tracker tied to its own brand. The company also failed to defend its software and became a third-party app, salvaging what it could through a deal to codevelop a version of the Apple Watch. Like many other traditional, vertically integrated firms, Nike was slow to recognize the inevitable, and thus it lost its chance to orchestrate the wearables ecosystem.

Apple's success with the iPhone, in contrast, was fueled by the company's recognition, in 2008, that its original strategy of providing all the phone's apps was wrong. Steve Jobs—who was initially opposed to non-Apple app providers—made an impressive U-turn, creating the iPhone App Store. This both allowed the firm to share revenue from apps sold and encouraged others to find ways to leverage the phone.

Participating in an ecosystem requires an outward-facing culture and the ability to manage relationships with a host of complementors. Those skills don't come easily to established players, which tend to default to one of two approaches: to create a vertically integrated, tightly controlled network, as Nokia did, or to hop on the bandwagon of open innovation and production, providing only a platform and leaving ecosystem management up to users. The risk there is that without some central impetus or incentive from the host, other parties may fail to engage. That happened with Watson, IBM's AI developer platform: Initial developer enthusiasm did not translate into activity and engagement.

There really aren't any default strategies for building an ecosystem. You need to decide carefully where and how to open up and then do so in a way that fits your competitive environment. Nest got this right: Concerned that by opening up the alarm function it would compromise its ability to control the home, it made a strategic decision to engage in alarm and monitoring itself rather than link up with Alarm.com or Honeywell. It invited complementors in other, nonstrategic areas instead. For its part, when Alarm.com entered the thermostat market, it chose to enable Nest connectivity; having a smaller installed base and less muscle than Google, it placed a premium on the ability to infiltrate more houses, more effectively, even if that reduced its aspirations for control.

Moving beyond strategy, to build an ecosystem you will need to manage your organization. The old part of it—that which currently generates revenue—will want to keep innovation under the firm's control and will treat complementors with suspicion, whereas the new parts will need to be externally focused. Big firms often separate the two parts, regarding the core as a margin-preserving inertial supertanker and hoping that a small fleet of "speedboats," some of which manage ecosystems, will pull the firm forward. Banks and insurance companies, for instance, often try to preserve their legacy structures and IT systems, hoping that a few add-ons will bring them into the digital, ecosystem-enabled age. But to succeed, ecosystems must be more closely aligned with the core.

New organizational structures are emerging that are better suited than traditional ones to these challenges. One example is the Chinese manufacturer Haier's *rendanheyi* model. Haier is organized around independently managed "microenterprises" that it may or may not own. IT facilitates information and data flows across the microenterprise units, each of which becomes, in a sense, an internal ecosystem with relatively porous boundaries, enabling the firm as a whole to position itself in a broader ecosystem.

5. How Many Ecosystems Should You Manage?

Some successful orchestrators manage a number of synergistic ecosystems, each covering a different part of the business and leading to a different path for expansion.

The Chinese tech giant Alibaba grew by creating an expanding set of connected ecosystems, starting in one market and shifting to others as it capitalized on customer information and refined its understanding of customer needs. It began with 1688.com (a wholesale marketplace), created Taobao (a C2C marketplace), moved into TMall (a third-party-seller B2C ecosystem), and expanded to Juhuasuan (a sales and marketing platform). And it is a part owner of Ant Financial, the world's most valuable fintech firm, which aims "to expand its ecosystem by penetrating more consumption scenarios in daily life."

The most obvious consequence of this dynamic is the growing dominance of national e-commerce and e-services by a small number of firms. In China, the almost equally huge Tencent and Baidu compete with Alibaba, which in many ways they resemble. Their Western equivalents are Google, Apple, Facebook, Amazon, and Microsoft. Aspiring to provide a unified service, these companies are shifting into ever more sectors, often through interfaces such as voice-activated assistants that appear seamless to the consumer. Mobility firms are doing similar things. Uber's expansion—think of Uber Eats and all the ventures of Uber Everything—demonstrates the company's ambition to integrate multiple ecosystems and manage the customer interface. Southeast Asian mobility firms such as Grab (Singapore) and Go-Jek (Indonesia) have gotten into payments as well, aiming to make themselves indispensable to the final customer.

As Marco Iansiti and Karim Lakhani recently noted, such hub firms are becoming formidable strategic bottlenecks that can direct the lion's share of value to themselves. But although it may seem that the future belongs to big, established firms with deep pockets and technological prowess, smaller upstarts (like Alibaba when it started, less than 20 years ago) and nontechnology firms have the potential to muscle in. The Chinese insurance and financial services conglomerate Ping An began by becoming more technologically savvy and soon ventured into adjacent areas, starting with health care and extending to lifestyle, in the process becoming the world's most valuable insurance group. It did so by creating focused ecosystems such as Ping An Good Doctor, which combines AI with physicians to provide medical advice, and Ping An Haofang, the country's largest online property platform. It has invested in Autohome, China's largest used-car marketplace, and in entertainment, through an alliance with Huayi Brothers. It then combined those verticals with some of its own units, including Ping An Bank and Zhong An insurance, to create the PingOne account: an offering that seeks to capture every customer interaction.

For complementors, different ecosystems represent different pathways to market—and most integrators are complementors in rivals' ecosystems (you'll find Microsoft Word in Android, Google Maps in Apple, Apple software in Microsoft systems, and so on). Firms choose to "multi-home" according to what specific ecosystems allow, the cost of redeploying in other ecosystems, and the benefits of cross-ecosystem customer reach.

A firm's role in one ecosystem may drive its participation in (or orchestration of) another, and there is plenty of room for strategizing. Samsung, the biggest user of the Android ecosystem—it sells more than 40% of Android phones—threatened to create a rival OS ecosystem if Google didn't make certain concessions. The companies reached a compromise, but they continue to compete over functions such as digital assistants, and the boundaries between Google's and Samsung's phone ecosystems continue to be hotly contested. Strategic interactions of this kind between firms and their associated ecosystems will only increase.

From Private Benefit to Public Good

The rise of ecosystem-based competition not only requires a new strategic framework and organizational model; it has significant implications for policy and regulation. In particular, the increasing success of integrators and their ability to become all-powerful orchestrators across an ever-growing number of ecosystems raises serious questions about a new form of market power.

Governments must strike a balance that both keeps their business environments healthy and safeguards their societies. Little global consensus has emerged about where that balance should lie. The rapid growth of many Chinese firms has relied on their unfettered ability to access data, while Europe sets tight restrictions on that activity. Will those limit economic growth in Europe relative to China? Maybe, but Europeans may consider the price worth paying, given the social benefits of privacy protections.

Whatever social priorities they set, all countries will need to change the analytical foundations of competition law, which has long focused on managing the market shares of individual firms.

As a recent report prepared for the UK Treasury argued, we need to adjust our approach to competition and regulation. In particular, we need to examine the terms of engagement in ecosystems, how orchestrators and integrators exert their power, what customer data those parties own, and how they interact with complementors. And while there is only one Apple, there are 2 million app developers. The fate of complementors may have more far-reaching societal effects than the high-profile fortunes of an orchestrator will have, and as we contemplate regulatory action, we must consider ecosystem governance, rules of engagement, and the well-being of the myriad, de facto weaker, complementors. We must also ask whether firms' desire to expand their reach and control an increasingly broad swath of activity restricts competition. To that end, the M&A of ecosystem plays should be scrutinized.

In approaching these challenges, policy makers should avoid the trap of treating all emerging ecosystems as commercial monsters in need of control. Ecosystems can provide new ways of bridging private benefit and public good. IDEO's CoLab circular economy portfolio advises firms in the textile and food sectors on reconfiguring their ecosystems to encourage the reuse of resources and the reduction of waste. Traipse's My Local Token provides localized digital currencies for U.S. downtowns that reinforce connections between residents and tourists on one hand and local businesses on the other. Velocia is creating a rewards ecosystem that encourages the use of public transit alongside on-demand services such as carpooling and carsharing to improve people's commutes. (Disclosure: I have advised all three of these companies.)

Business is undergoing a paradigm shift as a result of digital innovation: The very nature of competition is changing. Competing is increasingly about identifying new ways to collaborate and connect rather than simply offering alternative value propositions. But as the scope of opportunity expands, so too does the confusion of executives confronted with digital ecosystems. The complexity of those systems doesn't mean we should give up trying to make sense of them; it means we need to adjust. We must shift from rigid strategies based on prescriptive frameworks to dynamic experiments based on a process of inquiry. Start by asking yourself the five questions I've just proposed.

Originally published in September–October 2019. Reprint R1905J

Right Tech, Wrong Time

by Ron Adner and Rahul Kapoor

FOR THE PAST 30 YEARS, "creative destruction" has been a source of fascination at top-tier business schools and in magazines like this one. The almost obsessive interest in this topic is unsurprising, given the ever-changing, never-ending list of transformative threats—which today include the internet of things, 3-D printing, cloud computing, personalized medicine, alternative energy, and virtual reality.

Our understanding of the shifts that disrupt businesses, industries, and sectors has profoundly improved over the past 20 years: We know far more about how to identify those shifts and what dangers they pose to incumbent firms. But the *timing* of technological change remains a mystery. Even as some technologies and enterprises seem to take off overnight (ride sharing and Uber; social networking and Twitter), others take decades to unfold (high-definition TV, cloud computing). For firms and their managers, this creates a problem: Although we have become quite savvy about determining *whether* a new innovation poses a threat, we have very poor tools for knowing *when* such a transition will happen.

The number-one fear is being ready too late and missing the revolution (consider Blockbuster, which failed because it ignored the shift from video rentals to streaming). But the number-two fear should probably be getting ready too soon and exhausting resources before the revolution begins (think of any dot-com firm that died in the 2001 technology crash, only to see its ideas reborn later as a profitable Web 2.0 venture). This fear of acting prematurely applies both to established incumbents being threatened by disruptive change and to innovating start-ups carrying the flag of disruption.

To understand why some new technologies quickly supplant their predecessors while others catch on only gradually, we need to think about two things differently. First, we must look not just at the technology itself but also at the broader *ecosystem* that supports it. Second, we need to understand that competition may take place *between the new and the old ecosystems,* rather than between the technologies themselves. This perspective can help managers better predict the timing of transitions, craft more-coherent strategies for prioritizing threats and opportunities, and ultimately make wiser decisions about when and where to allocate organizational resources.

You're Only as Good as Your Ecosystem

Both established and disruptive initiatives depend on an array of complementary elements—technologies, services, standards, regulations—to deliver on their value propositions. The strength and maturity of the elements that make up the ecosystem play a key role in the success of new technologies—and the continued relevance of old ones.

The new technology's ecosystem

In assessing an emerging technology's potential, the paramount concern is whether it can satisfy customer needs and deliver value in a better way. To answer that question, investors and executives tend to drill down to specifics: How much additional development will be required before the technology is ready for commercial prime time? What will its production economics look like? Will it be price-competitive?

If the answers suggest that the new technology can really deliver on its promise, the natural expectation is that it will take over the market. Crucially, however, this expectation will hold only if the new technology's dependence on other innovations is low. For

Idea in Brief

The Problem

Over the past 20 years we've gotten very good at predicting whether a major new technology will supplant an older one—but we are still terrible at predicting when that substitution will take place.

The Insight

If the new technology doesn't need a new ecosystem to support it—if it is essentially plug-and-play—then adoption can be swift. But if other complements are needed, then the pace of substitution will slow until those challenges are resolved. Change takes even longer when the old technology gets a boost from improvements in its own ecosystem.

The Implications

Start-ups need to consider not just when their innovation will be viable, but also what external bottlenecks will arise. Incumbents, meanwhile, should use the transition period to up their own game—and to figure out a strategy for long-term survival.

example, a new lightbulb technology that can plug into an existing socket can deliver its promised performance right out of the box. In such cases, where the value proposition does not hinge on external factors, great product execution translates into great results.

However, many technologies do not fall into this plug-and-play mold. Rather, their ability to create value depends on the development and commercial deployment of other critical parts of the ecosystem. Consider HDTV, which could not gain traction until high-definition cameras, new broadcast standards, and updated production and postproduction processes also became commercially available. Until the entire ecosystem was ready, the technology revolution promised by HDTV was bound to be delayed, no matter how great its potential for a better viewing experience. For the pioneers who developed HDTV technology in the 1980s, being right about the vision brought little comfort during the 30 years it took for the rest of the ecosystem to emerge.

An improved lightbulb and an HDTV both depend on ecosystems of complementary elements. The difference is that the lightbulb plugs into an existing ecosystem (established power generation and distribution networks; wired homes), whereas the television requires the successful development of co-innovations. Improvements in the lightbulb will thus create immediate value for customers, but the TV's ability to create value is limited by the availability and progress of other elements in its ecosystem.

The old technology's ecosystem

Successful, established technologies—by definition—have overcome their emergence challenges and are embedded within successful, established ecosystems. Whereas new technologies can be held back by their ecosystems, incumbent technologies can be accelerated by improvements in theirs, even in the absence of progress in the core technology itself. For example, although the basic technology behind bar codes has not changed in decades, their utility improves every year as the IT infrastructure supporting them allows evermore information to be extracted. Hence in the 1980s, bar codes allowed prices to be automatically scanned into cash registers; in the 1990s, aggregating the bar code data from daily or weekly transactions provided insight into general inventory; in the modern era, bar code data is used for real-time inventory management and supply chain restocking. Similarly, improvements in DSL (digital subscriber line) technology have extended the life of copper telephone lines, which can now offer download speeds of 15 megabytes per second, making copper-wire services competitive with newer cable and fiber networks.

The War Between Ecosystems

When a new technology isn't a simple plug-and-play substitution—when it requires significant developments in the ecosystem in order to be useful—then a race between the new- and the old-technology ecosystems begins.

What determines who wins? For the *new* technology, the key factor is how quickly its ecosystem becomes sufficiently developed for users to realize the technology's potential. In the case of cloud-based applications and storage, for example, success depended not just on figuring out how to manage data in server farms, but also on

About the Research

WE DEVELOPED AND EXPLORED the ideas described in this article during a five-year research project on the pace of substitution in the semiconductor-manufacturing ecosystem.

The semiconductor industry's remarkably robust progress over the past 60 years was made possible by innovations in the lithography technology that semiconductor manufacturers use. We studied the successive generations of lithography equipment and noticed a pattern: In some cases, the new technology dominated the market in a matter of two to five years, whereas in other cases it faced prolonged, unexpected delays in achieving market dominance—and sometimes never did. This was true despite the fact that each generation offered superior performance, even on a price-adjusted performance basis.

To test our hypotheses about how ecosystem emergence challenges and extension opportunities affect the pace of substitution, we first collected and analyzed detailed data on every product and firm involved in every generation of the technology. We supplemented that information with extensive interviews with executives from firms throughout the ecosystem.

Our statistical analysis showed that 48% of the variation in the pace of substitution was attributable to traditional factors: price-adjusted performance differences, the number of rivals in the market, and the tenure of the old technology. When we added consideration of the ecosystem dynamics discussed in the article, we were able to account for a remarkable 82% of the variance.

For more details on the research, see "Innovation Ecosystems and the Pace of Substitution: Re-examining Technology S-Curves," by Ron Adner and Rahul Kapoor, *Strategic Management Journal* (March 2015).

ensuring the satisfactory performance of critical complements such as broadband and online security. For the *old* technology, what's important is how its competitiveness can be increased by improvement in the established ecosystem. In the case of desktop storage systems (the technology that cloud-based applications would replace), extension opportunities have historically included faster interfaces and more-robust components. As these opportunities become exhausted, we can expect substitution to accelerate.

Thus the pace of substitution is determined by the rate at which the new technology's ecosystem can overcome its emergence challenges relative to the rate at which the old technology's ecosystem can exploit its extension opportunities. To consider the interplay between these forces, we have developed a framework to help managers assess how quickly disruptive change is coming to their industry (see the chart "A framework for analyzing the pace of technology substitution"). There are four possible scenarios: creative destruction, robust resilience, robust coexistence, and the illusion of resilience.

Creative destruction

When the ecosystem emergence challenge for the new technology is low and the ecosystem extension opportunity for the old technology is also low (quadrant 1 in the framework), the new technology can be expected to achieve market dominance in short order (see point A in the exhibit "How fast does new technology replace the old?"). The new technology's ability to create value is not held back by bottlenecks elsewhere in the ecosystem, and the old technology has limited potential to improve in response to the threat. This quadrant aligns with concept of creative destruction—the idea that an innovative upstart can swiftly cause the demise of established competitors. While the old technology can continue serving niches for a long time (see "Bold Retreat," by Ron Adner and Daniel C. Snow, HBR, March 2010), the bulk of the market will abandon it relatively quickly in favor of the new technology. As an example, consider the rapid replacement of dot matrix printers by inkjet printers.

Robust resilience

When the balance is reversed—when the new technology's ecosystem confronts serious emergence challenges and the old technology's ecosystem has strong opportunities to improve (quadrant 4)—the pace of substitution will be very slow. The old technology can be expected to maintain a prosperous leadership position for an extended period. This quadrant is most consistent with technologies that seem revolutionary when they're first touted but appear overhyped in retrospect.

Bar codes and radio frequency identification (RFID) chips provide a good example. RFID chips hold the promise of storing far richer

A framework for analyzing the pace of technology substitution

The pace of substitution is determined by how quickly the new technology's ecosystem challenges are resolved and whether the old technology can exploit ecosystem opportunities for extension.

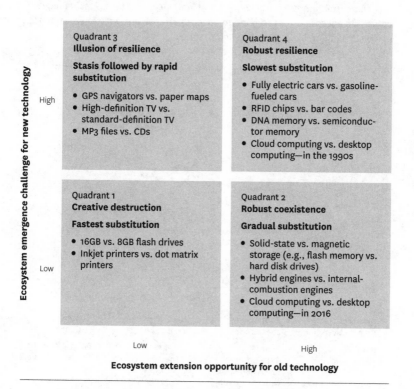

Quadrant 3
Illusion of resilience

Stasis followed by rapid substitution

- GPS navigators vs. paper maps
- High-definition TV vs. standard-definition TV
- MP3 files vs. CDs

Quadrant 4
Robust resilience

Slowest substitution

- Fully electric cars vs. gasoline-fueled cars
- RFID chips vs. bar codes
- DNA memory vs. semiconductor memory
- Cloud computing vs. desktop computing—in the 1990s

Quadrant 1
Creative destruction

Fastest substitution

- 16GB vs. 8GB flash drives
- Inkjet printers vs. dot matrix printers

Quadrant 2
Robust coexistence

Gradual substitution

- Solid-state vs. magnetic storage (e.g., flash memory vs. hard disk drives)
- Hybrid engines vs. internal-combustion engines
- Cloud computing vs. desktop computing—in 2016

Ecosystem emergence challenge for new technology — High / Low

Ecosystem extension opportunity for old technology — Low / High

data than bar codes ever could, but their adoption has lagged because of the slow deployment of suitable IT infrastructure and non-uniform industry standards. Meanwhile, IT improvements have extended the usability of bar code data, as we've already discussed, relegating RFID to niche applications and keeping the RFID revolution at bay for the past two decades. It may well be that RFID does eventually overcome its challenges and that ecosystem extension opportunities dry up for bar codes. If this happens, the dynamics

How fast does new technology replace the old?

Traditionally the substitution of a new technology for an old one is shown with two S curves (the solid lines). A more holistic view adds two more dynamics. First, if the new technology depends on the emergence of a new ecosystem, it becomes dominant more slowly (dotted line). Second, the old technology's competitiveness is extended if it can benefit from performance improvements in its surrounding ecosystem (dashed line).

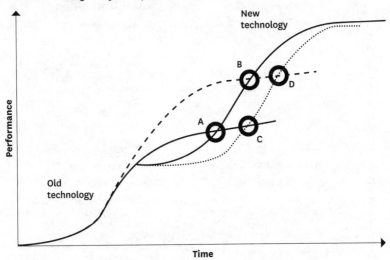

Creative destruction	Robust coexistence	Illusion of resilience	Robust resilience
Point A	**Point B**	**Point C**	**Point D**
The classic—and fastest—substitution takes place when the new technology's ecosystem is ready to go and the old technology's ecosystem can't be significantly improved.	If the new technology is compatible with the existing ecosystem and the old technology's ecosystem can be significantly improved, substitution takes place later (relative to creative destruction) and at a higher performance level.	If the new technology's ecosystem needs considerable development and the old technology's ecosystem has little room for improvement, the changeover occurs after time has passed without performance gains.	If the new technology's ecosystem needs considerable development and there are abundant opportunities to improve the old technology's ecosystem, the substitution occurs after the longest period of time and at the highest performance level.

Note: The exact positions of B and C will depend on the specifics of the case, but they will reflect an intermediate pace of substitution (relative to points A and D) and intermediate performance at substitution.

will shift from quadrant 4 to another quadrant, and the pace of substitution will quicken. But that will be small consolation to the firms and investors that committed to RFID decades ago. The opportunity cost of waiting for the rest of the system to catch up can mean that being in the right place 10 years too soon is more costly than missing the revolution completely.

When substitution is slow, there are also implications for the new technology's required performance levels (see point D in the exhibit). Every time IT improvements make bar codes more useful, for example, the quality threshold for the RFID technology is raised. Thus performance expectations for the innovation keep ratcheting upward, even as its wide adoption is held back by the underdeveloped state of its ecosystem.

Robust coexistence

When the ecosystem emergence challenge for the new technology is low and the ecosystem extension opportunity for the old technology is high (quadrant 2), competition will be robust. The new technology will make inroads into the market, but improvements in the old-technology ecosystem will allow the incumbent to defend its market share. There will be a prolonged period of coexistence. Although extension opportunities are unlikely to reverse the rise of the new technology, they will materially delay its dominance.

An instructive example is the competition between hybrid (gas-electric) automobile engines and traditional internal-combustion engines. Unlike fully electric engines, which need a supporting network of charging stations, hybrids were not held back by ecosystem emergence challenges. At the same time, however, traditional gas engines have become more fuel-efficient, and the ecosystem for the traditional technology has improved, too, as gas engines have become better integrated with other elements in the vehicle, such as heating and cooling systems.

A period of robust coexistence can be quite attractive from a consumer perspective. Performance of both ecosystems is improving—and the better the old technology's ecosystem becomes, the higher the performance bar is for the new technology's ecosystem (point B in the exhibit).

The illusion of resilience

When the ecosystem emergence challenge is high for the new technology and the ecosystem extension opportunity is low for the old technology (quadrant 3), not much will change until the emergence challenge is resolved—but then substitution will be rapid (point C in the exhibit). Examples here are HDTVs versus traditional TVs, and e-books versus printed books. Both of those revolutions were delayed not by advances in the old technology's ecosystem but by ecosystem-emergence challenges in the new technology.

In scenarios in this quadrant, an industry analysis will most likely show that the old technology maintains high market share, but growth has stalled. Because rapid market-share inversion is to be expected once the new technology fulfills its value creation potential, the dominance of the old technology is fragile. It is maintained not by continued progress in the old technology but by setbacks for the new competitor.

Implications for Action

Once you understand that in the race to dominance, ecosystems are just as important as technologies, you will be better at thinking through how quickly change is going to occur—and deciding what level of performance you need to aim for in the meantime. We will consider how to tackle these questions shortly, but first let's review a few general truths that emerge from this perspective.

- If your company is introducing a potentially transformative innovation, the full value will not be realized until all bottlenecks in the ecosystem are resolved. It may pay to focus a little less on perfecting the technology itself and a little more on resolving the most pressing problems in the ecosystem.

- If you are a threatened incumbent, it pays to analyze not just the emerging technology itself but also the ecosystem that supports it. The greater the ecosystem-emergence challenge for the new technology, the more time you have to strengthen your own performance.

- Strengthening incumbent performance may mean improving the old technology—but it can just as easily mean improving aspects of the ecosystem that supports it.

- Every time the old technology's performance gets better, the performance threshold for the new technology goes up.

With that overview in mind, let's look at how to use this framework to analyze your own technology strategy. We recommend having executive conversations focused on two questions: Which quadrant is our industry in? and What are the implications for our resource allocation and other strategic choices?

Which quadrant are we in?

Without the benefit of hindsight, your response to this question is clearly a matter of judgment. Some people would look at electric vehicles in 2016 and say they are still stuck in quadrant 4 (where we have placed them in our framework), pointing out that the charging infrastructure and battery performance are insufficient for mainstream adoption. Other people would position EVs on the cusp of quadrant 2, claiming that acceptance is growing and that better batteries make it possible to drive longer distances before recharging. Still others would place EVs solidly in quadrant 2, arguing that Tesla's success in selling its vehicles and populating its waiting lists is a sure sign that commercial potential is no longer constrained.

The sidebar "How Big a Threat Is the New Technology?" suggests issues to think through as you debate which quadrant you're in. Some questions pertain to the new technology and some to the old—but you will want to consider them all, regardless of whether you are an incumbent or a start-up. Don't expect all individual team members to agree on the answers to these questions. It is precisely by going through the process of articulating different views that teams can make the most of their collective insights.

How Big a Threat Is the New Technology?

PREDICTING THE PACE OF SUBSTITUTION requires analyzing the competition between the new- and the old-technology ecosystems. Six questions can help innovators and incumbents assess their positions and strategies.

New-Technology Questions

These questions (drawn from *The Wide Lens,* by coauthor Ron Adner) address the emergence challenges that confront the new technology. The answers should help innovators decide how to adjust their strategies.

1. What is the *execution risk*—the level of difficulty in delivering the focal innovation to the market on time and to spec?

2. What is the *co-innovation risk*—the extent to which the success of the new technology depends on the successful commercialization of other innovations?

3. What is the *adoption-chain risk*—the extent to which other partners need to adopt and adapt to the new technology before end consumers can fully assess its value proposition?

The greater the extent to which the new technology is facing any of these risks, the greater the challenge to be overcome, and the longer the expected delay in adoption of the technology.

Old-Technology Questions

These questions address the prospects for improving the competitiveness of the incumbent technology. The answers should help incumbents identify opportunities they might exploit.

1. Can the competitiveness of the old technology be extended by further improvements to the technology itself?

2. Can it be extended by improvements to complementary elements in its ecosystem?

3. Can it be extended by borrowing from innovations in the new technology and its ecosystem?

The more positive the reply to each of these questions, the greater the extension opportunity for the old technology.

What are the implications for resource allocation and other strategic choices?

Each quadrant in the framework carries different implications for resource allocation decisions. And since markets are not transformed all at once, the quadrant also suggests possible ways to position yourself during the transition.

In quadrant 1 (creative destruction), with the old technology stagnant and the new technology unhampered, innovators should aggressively invest in the new technology. Incumbents should follow the familiar prescriptions for embracing change to withstand the winds of creative destruction. Part of that is looking for niche positions where they can survive in the long term with the old technology. For example, pagers were largely replaced by cell phones, but they are still used by emergency-service providers.

In quadrant 2 (robust coexistence), incumbent firms can continue to invest in the old technology and aggressively invest in improvements to the ecosystem, knowing that the new and the old technologies will coexist for an extended period. As in quadrant 1, they should also seek niche positions for the old technology for the long term, but there is less urgency to do so. New-technology innovators should move full speed ahead on perfecting the new technology along with its complements. That includes testing and refining the offering with early adopters and segments that are potentially receptive.

In quadrant 3 (the illusion of resilience), new-technology champions should direct resources toward resolving their ecosystem challenges and developing complementary elements, and resist overprioritizing further development of the technology itself. When the bottleneck to adoption is the ecosystem, not the technology, pushing technology progress is pushing the wrong lever. Incumbents, for their part, must guard against the false assumption that they are maintaining their market position because of the merits of their own technology. As publishers of road atlases will attest, this is probably a time to harvest and make only incremental improvements, with an eye toward sunset; it is not the time to redouble innovation efforts in the old technology.

Finally, in quadrant 4 (robust resilience), incumbent firms should invest aggressively in upgrading their offerings and actively raising the bar that challengers need to cross. Obviously, new-technology innovators should be clear-eyed about working to resolve the ecosystem constraints they face. But at the same time they must recognize that the performance threshold for their core technology is rising. That necessitates both a significant level of resource investment and considerable patience regarding investment returns. Innovators are not likely to transform the sector in the foreseeable future, and therefore they will want to think through the economics of serving those customers they can succeed with.

One final note about the dynamics of change. Every innovator wants to end up in quadrant 1 so that it can play the classic creative-destruction game. But there are different paths for getting there. A hypothesis that predicts a transition path from Q4 to Q3 to Q1 is a bet on the exhaustion of the old technology. For an innovator, that would mean focusing on aligning the new-technology ecosystem without great concern for extending a performance advantage. In contrast, a predicted path of Q4 to Q2 to Q1 would mean competing against an improving incumbent-technology ecosystem. Here the innovator needs to continually elevate its performance while it simultaneously perfects the ecosystem.

Few modern firms are untouched by the urgency of innovation. But when it comes to strategizing for a revolution, the question of "whether" often drowns out the question of "when." Unfortunately, getting the first right but not the second can be devastating. "Right tech, wrong time" syndrome is a nightmare for any innovating firm. Closer analysis of the enabling contexts of rival technologies—Is the new ecosystem ready to roll? Does the old ecosystem still hold potential for improvement?—sheds more light on the question of timing. And better timing, in turn, will improve the efficiency and effectiveness of the innovation efforts that are so critical for survival and success.

Further Reading

FOR MORE INSIGHTS INTO THE relationship between technologies and their ecosystems, see the following:

- **"Match Your Innovation Strategy to Your Innovation Ecosystem,"** Ron Adner, HBR, April 2006

- **"A Sad Lesson in Collaborative Innovation,"** Ron Adner, HBR.org, May 9, 2012

- *The Wide Lens: What Successful Innovators See That Others Miss,* Ron Adner, Portfolio/Penguin 2013

- **"Beware of Old Technologies' Last Gasps,"** Daniel Snow, HBR, January 2008

- **"Value Creation in Innovation Ecosystems: How the Structure of Technological Interdependence Affects Firm Performance in New Technology Generations,"** Ron Adner and Rahul Kapoor, *Strategic Management Journal,* March 2010

Originally published in November 2016. Reprint R1611C

Managing Our Hub Economy

by Marco Iansiti and Karim R. Lakhani

THE GLOBAL ECONOMY IS COALESCING around a few digital super-powers. We see unmistakable evidence that a winner-take-all world is emerging in which a small number of "hub firms"—including Alibaba, Alphabet/Google, Amazon, Apple, Baidu, Facebook, Microsoft, and Tencent—occupy central positions. While creating real value for users, these companies are also capturing a disproportionate and expanding share of the value, and that's shaping our collective economic future. The very same technologies that promised to democratize business are now threatening to make it more monopolistic.

Beyond dominating individual markets, hub firms create and control essential connections in the networks that pervade our economy. Google's Android and related technologies form "competitive bottlenecks"; that is, they own access to billions of mobile consumers that other product and service providers want to reach. Google can not only exact a toll on transactions but also influence the flow of information and the data collected. Amazon's and Alibaba's marketplaces also connect vast numbers of users with large numbers of retailers and manufacturers. Tencent's WeChat messaging platform aggregates a billion global users and provides a critical source of consumer access for businesses offering online banking, entertainment, transportation, and other services. The more users who join these networks, the more attractive (and even necessary) it becomes for enterprises to offer their products and services through them. By driving increasing returns to scale and controlling crucial competitive bottlenecks, these digital superpowers can become even mightier, extract disproportionate value, and tip the global competitive balance.

Hub firms don't compete in a traditional fashion—vying with existing products or services, perhaps with improved features or lower cost. Rather, they take the network-based assets that have already reached scale in one setting and then use them to enter another industry and "re-architect" its competitive structure—transforming it from product-driven to network-driven. They plug adjacent industries into the same competitive bottlenecks they already control.

For example, the Alibaba spin-off Ant Financial does not simply offer better payment services, a better credit card, or an improved investment management service; it builds on data from Alibaba's already vast user base to commoditize traditional financial services and reorganize a good chunk of the Chinese financial sector around the Ant Financial platform. The three-year-old service already has over half a billion users and plans to expand well beyond China. Similarly, Google's automotive strategy does not simply entail creating an improved car; it leverages technologies and data advantages (many already at scale from billions of mobile consumers and millions of advertisers) to change the structure of the auto industry itself. (Disclosure: Both of us work or have worked with some of the firms mentioned in this article.)

If current trends continue, the hub economy will spread across more industries, further concentrating data, value, and power in the hands of a small number of firms employing a tiny fraction of the workforce. Disparity in firm valuation and individual wealth already causes widespread resentment. Over time, we can expect consumers, regulators, and even social movements to take an increasingly hostile stand against this concentration of value and economic connectivity. In a painfully ironic turn, after creating unprecedented opportunity across the global economy, digitization—and the trends it has given rise to—could exacerbate already dangerous levels of income inequality, undermine the economy, and even lead to social instability.

Idea in Brief

The Situation

A few digital superpowers, or hub firms, are capturing a disproportionate and growing share of the value being created in the global economy.

The Challenge

This trend threatens to exacerbate already dangerous levels of income inequality, undermine the economy, and destabilize society.

The Answer

While there are ways for companies that depend on hubs to defend their positions, the hubs themselves will have to do more to share economic value and sustain stakeholders.

Can these trends be reversed? We believe not. The "hub economy," as we will argue, is here to stay. But most companies will not become hubs, and they will need to respond astutely to the growing concentration of hub power. Digitizing operating capabilities will not be enough. Digital messaging platforms, for example, have already dealt a blow to telecom service providers; investment advisors still face threats from online financial-services companies. To remain competitive, companies will need to use their assets and capabilities differently, transform their core businesses, develop new revenue opportunities, and identify areas that can be defended from encroaching hub firms and others rushing in from previously disconnected economic sectors. Some companies have started on this path—Comcast, with its new Xfinity platform, is a notable example—but the majority, especially those in traditional sectors, still need to master the implications of network competition.

Most importantly, the very same hub firms that are transforming our economy must be part of the solution—and their leaders must step up. As Mark Zuckerberg articulated in his Harvard commencement address in May 2017, "we have a level of wealth inequality that hurts everyone." Business as usual is not a good option. Witness the public concern about the roles that Facebook and Twitter played in the recent U.S. presidential election, Google's challenges with global regulatory bodies, criticism of Uber's culture and operating policies, and complaints that Airbnb's rental practices are racially discriminatory and harmful to municipal housing stocks, rents, and pricing.

Thoughtful hub strategies will create effective ways to share economic value, manage collective risks, and sustain the networks and communities we all ultimately depend on. If carmakers, major retailers, or media companies continue to go out of business, massive economic and social dislocation will ensue. And with governments and public opinion increasingly attuned to this problem, hub strategies that foster a more stable economy and united society will drive differentiation among the hub firms themselves.

We are encouraged by Facebook's response to the public outcry over "fake news"—hiring thousands of dedicated employees, shutting down tens of thousands of phony accounts, working with news sources to identify untrue claims, and offering guides for spotting false information. Similarly, Google's YouTube division invests in engineering, artificial intelligence, and human resources and collaborates with NGOs to ensure that videos promoting political extremists and terrorists are taken down promptly.

A real opportunity exists for hub firms to truly lead our economy. This will require hubs to fully consider the long-term societal impact of their decisions and to prioritize their ethical responsibilities to the large economic ecosystems that increasingly revolve around them. At the same time, the rest of us—whether in established enterprises or start-ups, in institutions or communities—will need to serve as checks and balances, helping to shape the hub economy by providing critical, informed input and, as needed, pushback.

The Digital Domino Effect

The emergence of economic hubs is rooted in three principles of digitization and network theory. The first is Moore's law, which states that computer processing power will double approximately every two years. The implication is that performance improvements will continue driving the augmentation and replacement of human activity with digital tools. This affects any industry that has integrated computers into its operations—which pretty much covers the entire economy. And advances in machine learning and cloud computing have only reinforced this trend.

The second principle involves connectivity. Most computing devices today have built-in network connectivity that allows them to communicate with one another. Modern digital technology enables the sharing of information at near-zero marginal cost, and digital networks are spreading rapidly. Metcalfe's law states that a network's value increases with the number of nodes (connection points) or users—the dynamic we think of as network effects. This means that digital technology is enabling significant growth in value across our economy, particularly as open-network connections allow for the recombination of business offerings, such as the migration from payment tools to the broader financial services and insurance that we've seen at Ant Financial.

But while value is being created for everyone, value capture is getting more skewed and concentrated. This is because in networks, traffic begets more traffic, and as certain nodes become more heavily used, they attract additional attachments, which further increases their importance. This brings us to the third principle, a lesser-known dynamic originally posited by the physicist Albert-László Barabási: the notion that digital-network formation naturally leads to the emergence of positive feedback loops that create increasingly important, highly connected hubs. As digital networks carry more and more economic transactions, the economic power of network hubs, which connect consumers, firms, and even industries to one another, expands. Once a hub is highly connected (and enjoying increasing returns to scale) in one sector of the economy (such as mobile telecommunications), it will enjoy a crucial advantage as it begins to connect in a new sector (automobiles, for example). This can, in turn, drive more and more markets to tip, and the many players competing in traditionally separate industries get winnowed down to just a few hub firms that capture a growing share of the overall economic value created—a kind of digital domino effect.

This phenomenon isn't new. But in recent years, the high degree of digital connectivity has dramatically sped up the transformation. Just a few years ago, cell phone manufacturers competed head-to-head for industry leadership in a traditional product market without appreciable network effects. Competition led to innovation and differentiation, with a business model delivering healthy profitability at scale for a dozen or so major competitors. But with the introduction of iOS and Android, the industry began to tip away from its hardware centricity to network structures centered on these multisided platforms. The platforms connected smartphones to a large number of apps and services. Each new app makes the platform it sits on more valuable, creating a powerful network effect that in turn creates a more daunting barrier to entry for new players. Today Motorola, Nokia, BlackBerry, and Palm are out of the mobile phone business, and Google and Apple are extracting the lion's share of the sector's value. The value captured by the large majority of complementors—the app developers and third-party manufacturers—is generally modest at best.

The domino effect is now spreading to other sectors and picking up speed. Music has already tipped to Apple, Google, and Spotify. E-commerce is following a similar path: Alibaba and Amazon are gaining more share and moving into traditional brick-and-mortar strongholds like groceries (witness Amazon's acquisition of Whole Foods). We've already noted the growing power of WeChat in messaging and communications; along with Facebook and others, it's challenging traditional telecom service providers. On-premise computer and software offerings are losing ground to the cloud services provided by Amazon, Microsoft, Google, and Alibaba. In financial services, the big players are Ant, Paytm, Ingenico, and the independent start-up Wealthfront; in home entertainment, Amazon, Apple, Google, and Netflix dominate.

Where are powerful hub firms likely to emerge next? Health care, industrial products, and agriculture are three contenders. But let's examine how the digital domino effect could play out in another prime candidate, the automotive sector, which in the United States alone provides more than seven million jobs and generates close to a trillion dollars in yearly sales.

Re-architecting the Automotive Sector

As with many other products and services, cars are now connected to digital networks, essentially becoming rolling information and transaction nodes. This connectivity is reshaping the structure of the automotive industry. When cars were merely products, car sales were the main prize. But a new source of value is emerging: the connection to consumers in transit. Americans spend almost an hour, on average, getting to and from work every day, and commutes keep getting longer. Auto manufacturers, responding to consumer demand, have already given hub firms access to dashboard screens in many cars; drivers can use Apple or Google apps on the car's built-in display instead of on their smartphones. If consumers embrace self-driving vehicles, that one hour of consumer access could be worth hundreds of billions of dollars in the U.S. alone.

Which companies will capitalize on the vast commercial potential of a new hour of free time for the world's car commuters? Hub firms like Alphabet and Apple are first in line. They already have bottleneck assets like maps and advertising networks at scale, and both are ready to create super-relevant ads pinpointed to the car's passengers and location. One logical add-on feature for autonomous vehicles would be a "Drive there" button that appears when an ad pops up (as already happens on Google's Waze app); pressing it would order the car to head to the touted destination.

In a future when people are no longer behind the wheel, cars will become less about the driving experience and more about the apps and services offered by automobiles as they ferry passengers around. Apart from a minority of cars actually driven for fun, differentiation will lessen, and the vehicle itself might well become commoditized. That will threaten manufacturers' core business: The car features that buyers will care most about—software and networks—will be largely outside the automakers' control, and their price premiums will go down.

The transformation will also upend a range of connected sectors—including insurance, automotive repairs and maintenance, road construction, law enforcement, and infrastructure—as the digital dominos continue to fall. (See the exhibit "The connected-car ecosystem.")

The connected-car ecosystem

Three software platforms—Android Auto, Apple CarPlay, and, to a lesser extent, OpenCar—dominate the market for integrating smartphone functionality into vehicles. They constitute powerful bottleneck assets because they have scores of supply-chain partners (left) and they enable other stakeholders (right) to reach consumers. (Note: The companies, apps, and regulators listed are selected examples only.)

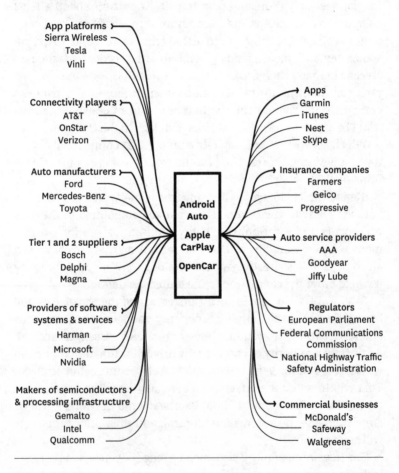

App platforms
Sierra Wireless
Tesla
Vinli

Connectivity players
AT&T
OnStar
Verizon

Auto manufacturers
Ford
Mercedes-Benz
Toyota

Tier 1 and 2 suppliers
Bosch
Delphi
Magna

Providers of software
systems & services
Harman
Microsoft
Nvidia

Makers of semiconductors
& processing infrastructure
Gemalto
Intel
Qualcomm

**Android
Auto

Apple
CarPlay

OpenCar**

Apps
Garmin
iTunes
Nest
Skype

Insurance companies
Farmers
Geico
Progressive

Auto service providers
AAA
Goodyear
Jiffy Lube

Regulators
European Parliament
Federal Communications
Commission
National Highway Traffic
Safety Administration

Commercial businesses
McDonald's
Safeway
Walgreens

For existing auto manufacturers, the picture is grim but not hopeless. Some companies are exploring a pay-per-use model for their cars and are acquiring, launching, or partnering with car-as-a-service providers. GM, for one, invested $500 million in the ride-sharing service Lyft, and its luxury-car division is now offering a monthly car subscription service. Daimler launched a car-sharing business called car2go. Several manufacturers have also invested in their own research into driverless vehicles or partnered with external providers.

Beyond these business-model experiments, automakers will need to play as the hubs do, by participating in the platform competition that will determine value capture in the sector. At least for the moment, alternatives to Google and Apple are scarce. One example is OpenCar, recently acquired by Inrix, a traditional auto supplier. Unlike Apple CarPlay and Google's Android Auto, which limit automaker-specific customization and require access to proprietary car data, the OpenCar framework is fully controlled by the car manufacturer. To take on the established giants, we believe that OpenCar and Inrix will have to develop an effective advertising or commerce platform or adopt some other indirect monetization strategy—and to do that, they'll probably need to partner with companies that have those capabilities.

To reach the scale required to be competitive, automotive companies that were once fierce rivals may need to join together. Here Technologies, which provides precision mapping data and location services, is an interesting example. Here has its roots in Navteq, one of the early online mapping companies, which was first bought by Nokia and later acquired by a consortium of Volkswagen, BMW, and Daimler (the multibillion-dollar price tag may have been too high for any single carmaker to stomach). Here provides third-party developers with sophisticated tools and APIs for creating location-based ads and other services. The company represents an attempt by auto manufacturers to assemble a "federated" platform and, in doing so, neutralize the threat of a potential competitive bottleneck controlled by Google and Apple. The consortium could play a significant role in preventing automotive value capture from tipping completely toward existing hub firms.

Of course, successful collaboration depends on a common, strongly felt commitment. So as traditional enterprises position themselves for a fight, they must understand how the competitive dynamics in their industries have shifted.

Increasing Returns to Scale Are Hard to Beat

Competitive advantage in many industries is moderated by *decreasing* returns to scale. In traditional product and service businesses, the value creation curve typically flattens out as the number of consumers increases, as we see in the exhibit "Profiting from a growing customer base." A firm gains no particular advantage as its user base continues to increase beyond already efficient levels, which enables multiple competitors to coexist.

Profiting from a growing customer base

For traditional product and service businesses, gaining additional customers does not continue adding commensurate value after a certain point. However, many platform businesses (Amazon, Facebook, and the like) become more and more valuable as more people and companies use them, connect with one another, and create network effects.

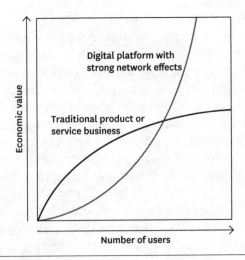

Some digital technologies, however, exhibit *increasing* returns to scale. A local advertising platform gets better and better as more and more users attract more and more ads. And as the number of ads increases, so does the ability to target the ads to the users, making individual ads more valuable. An advertising platform is thus similar to software platforms such as Windows, Linux, Android, and iOS, which exhibit increasing returns to scale—their growing value to consumers increases the number of available apps, while the value to app developers rises as the number of consumers rises. The more consumers, the greater the incentive for developers to build apps, and the more apps there are, the more motivated consumers are to use their digital devices.

These considerations are important to the nature of hub competition. The economics of traditional decreasing returns make it possible for several competitors to coexist and provide differentiated value to attract users. That's the dynamic in the auto industry today, with many car manufacturers competing with one another to offer a variety of differentiated products. But the increasing returns in digital assets like ad platforms (or possibly driverless-car technology) will heighten the advantage of the competitor with the largest scale, the largest network of users, or the most data. And this is where the hub firms will most likely leverage their large and growing lead—and cause value to concentrate around them.

In contrast with traditional product and service businesses, network-based markets exhibiting increasing returns to scale will, over time, tip toward a narrow set of players. This implies that if a conventional decreasing-returns business (say, telecom or media) is threatened by a new type of competitor whose business model experiences increasing returns, the conventional player is in for a rough ride. With increasing returns to scale, a digital technology can provide a bottleneck to an entire industrial sector. And left alone, competitive bottlenecks dramatically skew value capture away from traditional firms.

Pushing Back

Hub firms often compete against one another. Microsoft has made substantial investments in augmented reality in an effort to create a new hub and counterbalance the power that Google and Apple wield in the mobile space. Facebook acquired Oculus to force a similar structural shift in the emerging field of virtual reality. And a battle is looming in the smart-home arena, as Google, Apple, Microsoft, and Samsung attempt to reduce Amazon's early lead in voice-activated home technology.

But how does the rest of the economy deal with the increasing returns to scale of hub firms? With enough foresight and investment, traditional firms can resist by becoming hubs themselves, as we are seeing especially in the internet of things (IoT) space. GE is the classic example of this approach, with its investment in the Predix platform and the creation of GE Digital. (See the article "How I Remade GE," HBR, September–October 2017.) Other companies are following suit in different settings—for example, Verizon and Vodafone with their IoT platforms.

Firms can also shape competition by investing to ensure that there are multiple hubs in each sector—and even influencing which ones win. They can organize to support less-established platforms, thus making a particular hub more viable and an industry sector more competitive in the long term. Deutsche Telekom, for instance, is partnering with Microsoft Azure (rather than Amazon Web Services) for cloud computing in Central Europe.

Most importantly, the value generated by networks will change as firms compete, innovate, and respond to community and regulatory pressure. Multi-homing—a practice enabling participants on one hub's ecosystem to easily join another—can significantly mitigate the rise of hub power. For example, drivers and passengers routinely multi-home across different ride-sharing platforms, often checking prices on Uber, Lyft, and Fasten to see which is offering the best deal. Retailers are starting to multi-home across payment systems, supporting multiple solutions (such as Apple Pay, Google Wallet, and Samsung Pay). If multi-homing is common, the market is less likely to tip to a single player, preserving competition and diffusing value capture. Indeed, companies will need to make their products and services available on multiple hubs and encourage the formation of new hubs to avoid being held hostage by one dominant player. Take the wireless-speaker manufacturer Sonos: It has ensured that its music system seamlessly integrates with as many music services as possible, including Apple Music, Amazon Music Unlimited, Google Play Music, Pandora, Spotify, and Tidal.

Collective action can also restructure economic networks, shape value creation and capture, and ease competitive bottlenecks. In the 1990s the open-source community organized to compete against Microsoft Windows with the Linux operating system. That effort was actively supported by traditional players such as IBM and Hewlett-Packard and reinforced later by Google and Facebook. Today Linux (and Linux-related products) are firmly established in enterprises, consumer devices, and cloud computing. Similarly, the Mozilla open-source community and its Firefox browser broke Microsoft's grip on navigating the internet. Even Apple, notorious for its proprietary approach, relies on open-source software for its core operating systems and web services, and the infamous iPhone jailbreaking craze demonstrated both the extraordinary demand for third-party apps and the burgeoning supply of them.

Open source has grown beyond all expectations to create an increasingly essential legacy of common intellectual property, capabilities, and methodologies. Now collective action is going well beyond code sharing to include coordination on data aggregation, the use of common infrastructure, and the standardization of practices to further equilibrate the power of hubs. Efforts like OpenStreetMap are leading the way in maps, and Mozilla's Common Voice project is crowdsourcing global voice data to open up the speech-recognition bottleneck.

Collective action will be increasingly crucial to sustaining balance in the digital economy. As economic sectors coalesce into networks and as powerful hubs continue to form, other stakeholders will need to work together to ensure that hubs look after the interests of all network members. Cooperation will become more important for the rivals that orbit hubs; indeed, strategic joint action by companies that are not hubs may be the best competitive antidote to the rising power of hub firms.

The public is also raising concerns about privacy, online tracking, cybersecurity, and data aggregation. Solutions being suggested include requirements for social network and data portability similar to the requirements for phone number portability that telecommunications regulators instituted to increase competition among phone service providers.

The Ethics of Network Leadership

The responsibility for sustaining our (digital) economy rests partly with the same leaders who are poised to control it. By developing such central positions of power and influence, hub firms have become de facto stewards of the long-term health of our economy. Leaders of hub companies need to realize that their organizations are analogous to "keystone" species in biological ecosystems— playing a critical role in maintaining their surroundings. Apple, Alibaba, Alphabet/Google, Amazon, and others that benefit disproportionately from the ecosystems they dominate have rational and ethical reasons to support the economic vitality of not just their direct participants but also the broader industries they serve. In particular, we argue that hub companies need to incorporate value *sharing* into their business models, along with value creation and value capture.

Building and maintaining a healthy ecosystem is in the best interests of hub companies. Amazon and Alibaba claim millions of marketplace sellers, and they profit from every transaction those merchants make. Similarly, Google and Apple earn billions in revenue from the third-party apps that run on their platforms. Both companies already invest heavily in the developer community, providing programming frameworks, software tools, and opportunities and business models that enable developers to grow their businesses. But such efforts will need to be scaled up and refined as hub firms find themselves at the center of—and relying on—much larger and more-complex ecosystems. Preserving the strength and productivity of complementary communities should be a fundamental part of any hub firm's strategy.

Uber provides an interesting example of the repercussions of getting this wrong. Uber's viability depends on its relations with its drivers and riders, who have often criticized the company's practices. Under pressure from those communities—and from competitors that offer drivers the potential to earn more—Uber is making improvements. Still, its challenges suggest that no hub will maintain an advantage over the long term if it neglects the well-being of its ecosystem partners. Microsoft learned a hard lesson when it failed to maintain the health of its PC software ecosystem, losing out to the Linux community in cloud services.

But network ethics are not just about financial considerations; social concerns are equally important. Centralized platforms, such as Kiva for charitable impact investing and Airbnb for accommodation bookings, have been found to be susceptible to racial discrimination. In Airbnb's case, external researchers convincingly demonstrated that African American guests were especially likely to have their reservation requests rejected. The pressure is now on Airbnb to fight bias both by educating its proprietors and by modifying certain platform features. Additionally, as Airbnb continues to grow, it must work to ensure that its hosts heed municipal regulations, lest they face a potentially devastating regulatory backlash.

Indeed, if hubs do not promote the health and sustainability of the many firms and individuals in their networks, other forces will undoubtedly step in. Governments and regulators will increasingly act to encourage competition, protect consumer welfare, and foster economic stability. Consider the challenges Google faces in Europe, where regulators are concerned about the dominance of both its search advertising business and its Android platform.

The centralizing forces of digitization are not going to slow down anytime soon. The emergence of powerful hub firms is well under way, and the threats to global economic well-being are unmistakable. All actors in the economy—but particularly the hub firms themselves—should work to sustain the entire ecosystem and observe new principles, for both strategic and ethical reasons. Otherwise, we are all in serious trouble.

Originally published in September–October 2017. Reprint R1705F

Why Some Platforms Thrive . . . and Others Don't

by Feng Zhu and Marco Iansiti

IN 2016, DIDI BECAME THE WORLD'S LARGEST ride-sharing company, reaching 25 million trips a day in China and surpassing the combined daily trips of all other ride-sharing companies across the globe. It had arrived at this milestone by merging in 2015 with its domestic rival, Kuaidi, and pushing Uber out of the Chinese market after a fierce, expensive battle. With its competition gutted, Didi gradually began to improve its margins by reducing subsidies to drivers and passengers.

But just as the company began to reach profitability, in early 2018, Meituan, a giant player in online-to-offline services such as food delivery, movie ticketing, and travel booking, launched its own ride-hailing business in Shanghai. Meituan didn't charge drivers to use its platform for the first three months and afterward took only 8% of their revenues, while Didi took 20%. Drivers and passengers flocked to the new service. In April, Didi struck back by entering the food delivery market in Wuxi, a city close to Shanghai. What followed was a costly price war, with many meals being sold for next to nothing because of heavy subsidies from both companies. So much for Didi's profitability.

Didi was taking other hits too. In March 2018, Alibaba's mapping unit—Gaode Map, the largest navigation service in China—had started a carpooling business in Chengdu and Wuhan. It didn't charge drivers at all, and in July it began offering passengers the option of ordering from several ride-hailing services. Meanwhile, Ctrip, China's largest online travel service, had announced in April that it had been granted a license to provide car-hailing services across the country.

Why hadn't Didi's immense scale shut down its competition for ride services in China? Why wasn't this a winner-take-all market, as many analysts had predicted? Moreover, why do some platform businesses—such as Alibaba, Facebook, and Airbnb—flourish, while Uber, Didi, and Meituan, among others, hemorrhage cash? What enables digital platforms to fight off competition and grow profits?

To answer those questions, you need to understand the networks a platform is embedded in. The factors affecting the growth and sustainability of platform firms (and digital operating models generally) differ from those of traditional firms. Let's start with the fact that on many digital networks the cost of serving an additional user is negligible, which makes a business inherently easier to scale up. And because much of a network-based firm's operational complexity is outsourced to the service providers on the platform or handled by software, bottlenecks to value creation and growth usually aren't tied to human or organizational factors—another important departure from traditional models. Ultimately, in a digital network business, the employees don't deliver the product or service—they just design and oversee an automated, algorithm-driven operation. Lasting competitive advantage hinges more on the interplay between the platform and the network it orchestrates and less on internal, firm-level factors. In other words, in the digitally connected economy the long-term success of a product or service depends heavily on the health, defensibility, and dominance of the ecosystem in which it operates.

And as Didi is learning, it's often easier for a digital platform to achieve scale than to sustain it. After all, the advantages that allow the platform to expand quickly work for its competitors and anyone else who wants to get into the market. The reason that some platforms thrive while others struggle really lies in their ability to

Idea in Brief

The Challenge

It's easier for digital platforms to achieve scale than to maintain it.

The Reason

Five basic network properties shape their scalability, profitability, and ultimately their sustainability.

The Insight

Analysis of these properties will help entrepreneurs and investors understand platforms' prospects for long-term success.

---

manage five fundamental properties of networks: network effects, clustering, risk of disintermediation, vulnerability to multi-homing, and bridging to multiple networks.

Strength of Network Effects

The importance of network effects is well known. Economists have long understood that digital platforms like Facebook enjoy same-side ("direct") network effects: The more Facebook friends you have in your network, the more likely you are to attract additional friends through your friends' connections. Facebook also leverages cross-side ("indirect") network effects, in which two different groups of participants—users and app developers—attract each other. Uber can similarly mine cross-side effects, because more drivers attract more riders, and vice versa.

Less well acknowledged is the fact that the *strength* of network effects can vary dramatically and can shape both value creation and capture. When network effects are strong, the value provided by a platform continues to rise sharply with the number of participants. For example, as the number of users on Facebook increases, so does the amount and variety of interesting and relevant content. Video game consoles, however, exhibit only weak network effects, as we discovered in a research study. This is because video games are a hit-driven business, and a platform needs relatively few hits to be successful. The total number of game titles available isn't as important in console sales as having a few of the right games. Indeed, even an entrant with only a small technical advantage (and a good business development team) can steal significant market share from incumbents. That explains why in 2001 Microsoft's new Xbox posed such a threat to Sony's then-dominant PlayStation 2, and why each console has gone up and down in market share, alternately taking the lead, over the years.

Even more critically, the strength of network effects can change over time. Windows is a classic example. During the heyday of personal computers in the 1990s, most PC applications were "client based," meaning they actually lived on the computers. Back then, the software's network effects were strong: The value of Windows increased dramatically as the number of developers writing apps for it climbed, topping 6 million at the peak of its popularity. By the late 1990s Windows seemed entrenched as the leading platform. However, as internet-based apps, which worked across different operating systems, took off, the network effects of Windows diminished and barriers to entry fell, allowing Android, Chrome, and iOS operating systems to gain strength on PCs and tablets. Mac shipments had also begun to rise in the mid-2000s, increasing more than fivefold by the end of the decade. This turn of events illustrates that when an incumbent's network effects weaken, so does its market position.

It is possible for firms to design features that strengthen network effects, however. Amazon, for example, has built multiple types of effects into its business model over the years. In the beginning, Amazon's review systems generated same-side effects: As the number of product reviews on the site increased, users became more likely to visit Amazon to read the reviews as well as write them. Later, Amazon's marketplace, which allows third parties to sell products to Amazon users, generated cross-side network effects, in which buyers and third-party sellers attracted each other. Meanwhile, Amazon's recommendation system, which suggests products on the basis of past purchase behavior, amplified the impact of the company's scale by continually learning about consumers' preferences. The more consumers used the site, the more accurate the recommendations Amazon could provide them. While not usually recognized as a network effect per se, learning effects operate a lot like same-side effects and can increase barriers to entry.

Network Clustering

In a research project with Xinxin Li of the University of Connecticut and Ehsan Valavi, a doctoral student at Harvard Business School, we found that the structure of a network influences a platform business's ability to sustain its scale. The more a network is fragmented into local clusters—and the more isolated those clusters are from one another—the more vulnerable a business is to challenges. Consider Uber. Drivers in Boston care mostly about the number of riders in Boston, and riders in Boston care mostly about drivers in Boston. Except for frequent travelers, no one in Boston cares much about the number of drivers and riders in, say, San Francisco. This makes it easy for another ride-sharing service to reach critical mass in a local market and take off through a differentiated offer such as a lower price. Indeed, in addition to its rival Lyft at the national level, Uber confronts a number of local threats. For example, in New York City, Juno and Via, as well as local taxi companies, are giving it competition. Didi likewise faces a number of strong contenders in multiple cities.

Now let's compare Uber's market with Airbnb's. Travelers don't care much about the number of Airbnb hosts in their home cities; instead, they care about how many there are in the cities they plan to visit. Hence, the network more or less is one large cluster. Any real challenger to Airbnb would have to enter the market on a global scale—building brand awareness around the world to attract critical masses of travelers and hosts. So breaking into Airbnb's market becomes much more costly.

It's possible to strengthen a network by building global clusters on top of local clusters. While Craigslist, a classified ad site, primarily connects users and providers of goods and services in local markets, its housing and job listings attract users from other markets. Facebook's social games (like FarmVille) established new connections among players who were strangers, creating a denser, more global,

Which network structure is more defensible?

Some digital networks are fragmented into local clusters of users. In Uber's network, riders and drivers interact with network members outside their home cities only occasionally. But other digital networks are global; on Airbnb, visitors regularly connect with hosts around the world.

Platforms on global networks are much less vulnerable to challenges, because it's difficult for new rivals to enter a market on a global scale.

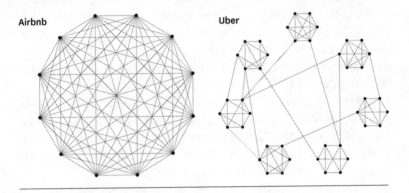

more integrated network, which is easier to defend from competition. Both Facebook and WeChat, a popular social-networking app in China, have been enhancing their networks by getting popular brands and celebrities—those with national and often international appeal—to create public accounts and post and interact with users.

Risk of Disintermediation

Disintermediation, wherein network members bypass a hub and connect directly, can be a big problem for any platform that captures value directly from matching or by facilitating transactions. Imagine that you hire a house cleaner from a platform like Homejoy and are satisfied with the service. Would you really go back to Homejoy to hire the same person again? If a user has found the right match, there's little incentive to return to the platform. Additionally, after obtaining enough clients from a platform to fill his or her schedule, the house cleaner won't need that platform anymore. This was exactly the problem that doomed Homejoy, which shut down in 2015, five years after it was founded.

Platforms have used various mechanisms to deter disintermediation, such as creating terms of service that prohibit users from conducting transactions off the platform, and blocking users from exchanging contact information. Airbnb, for example, withholds hosts' exact locations and phone numbers until payments are made. Such strategies aren't always effective, though. Anything that makes a platform more cumbersome to use can make it vulnerable to a competitor offering a streamlined experience.

Some platforms try to avoid disintermediation by enhancing the value of conducting business on them. They may facilitate transactions by providing insurance, payment escrow, or communication tools; resolve disputes; or monitor activities. But those services become less valuable once trust develops among platform users—and the strategies can backfire as the need for the platform decreases. One of us, Feng, and Grace Gu, a doctoral student at Harvard Business School, saw this effect in a study of an online freelance marketplace. As the platform improved its reputation-rating system, trust between clients and freelancers grew stronger, and disintermediation became more frequent, offsetting the revenue gains from better matching.

Some platforms address disintermediation risks by introducing different strategies for capturing value—with varying results. Thumbtack, a marketplace connecting consumers with local service providers such as electricians and guitar teachers, charges for lead generation: Customers post requests on the site, and service providers send them quotes and pay Thumbtack fees if those customers respond. That model captures value before the two sides even agree to work together and has helped save the company from withering like Homejoy. Thumbtack today is handling over $1 billion worth of transactions annually. The downside of its revenue model is that it doesn't prevent the two sides from building a long-term relationship outside the platform after a match.

Alibaba took a different approach with its Taobao e-commerce platform. When Taobao entered the market, in 2003, eBay's EachNet had more than 85% of the Chinese consumer-to-consumer market. However, Taobao didn't charge listing or transaction fees and even set up an instant-messaging service, Wangwang, that allowed buyers to ask questions directly of sellers and haggle with them in real time. In contrast, EachNet charged sellers transaction fees and, because it was concerned about disintermediation, didn't allow direct interactions between buyers and sellers until a sale had been confirmed. Not surprisingly, Taobao quickly took over leadership of the market, and at the end of 2006, eBay shut down its Chinese site. Taobao today continues to offer its C2C marketplace services free of charge and captures value through advertising revenues and sales of storefront software that helps merchants manage their online businesses.

After estimating that it could lose as much as 90% of its business to disintermediation, the Chinese outsourcing marketplace ZBJ, which launched in 2006 with a model of charging a 20% commission, began looking for new revenue sources. In 2014 it discovered that many new business owners used its site to get help with logo design. Typically, the next job those clients would need done was business and trademark registration, which the platform started to offer. Today ZBJ is the largest provider of trademark registration in China—a service that generates more than $70 million in annual revenue for the firm. The company has also significantly reduced its transaction fees and focused its resources on growing its user base instead of fighting disintermediation. As the experience of ZBJ, which is now valued at more than $1.5 billion, shows, when disintermediation is a threat, providing complementary services can work a lot better than charging transaction fees.

Vulnerability to Multi-Homing

Multi-homing happens when users or service providers (network "nodes") form ties with multiple platforms (or "hubs") at the same time. This generally occurs when the cost of adopting an additional platform is low. In the ride-hailing industry, many drivers and riders use both, say, Lyft and Uber—riders to compare prices and wait times, and drivers to reduce their idle time. Similarly, merchants often work with multiple group-buying sites, and restaurants with multiple food-delivery platforms. And even app developers, whose costs are not trivial, still find it makes sense to develop products for both iOS and Android systems.

When multi-homing is pervasive on each side of a platform, as it is in ride hailing, it becomes very difficult for a platform to generate a profit from its core business. Uber and Lyft are constantly undercutting each other as they compete for riders and drivers.

Incumbent platform owners can reduce multi-homing by locking in one side of the market (or even both sides). To encourage exclusivity, both Uber and Lyft gave bonuses in many markets to people who completed a certain number of trips in a row without rejecting or canceling any or going offline during peak hours. And while rides are in progress, both platforms provide drivers new requests for pickups very close to current passengers' drop-off locations, reducing the drivers' idle time and hence the temptation to use other platforms. Yet because of the inherently low cost of adopting multiple platforms, multi-homing is still rampant in ride sharing.

Attempts to prevent multi-homing can also have unintended side effects. In one research project, Feng and Hui Li of Carnegie Mellon University examined what happened in 2011 when Groupon retooled its deal counter—which tracks the amount of people who have signed up for a specific offer on its site—to show ambiguous ranges, rather than precise numbers. It then became more difficult for LivingSocial to identify and poach the popular merchants on Groupon. As a result, LivingSocial started to source more exclusive deals. While Groupon was able to reduce merchant-side multi-homing, the research found, consumers became more likely to visit both sites, because there were fewer overlapping deals on them, and it cost little to multi-home. That finding points to a key challenge platform firms face: Reducing multi-homing on one side of the market may increase multi-homing on the opposite side.

Other approaches seem to work better. Let's look again at the video game industry: Console makers often sign exclusive contracts with game publishers. On the platforms' user side, the high prices of consoles and subscription services, such as Xbox Live and PlayStation Plus, reduce players' incentives to multi-home. Lowering multi-homing on both sides of the market decreased competitive intensity and allowed the console makers to be profitable. Amazon, which provides fulfillment services to third-party sellers, charges them higher fees when their orders are not from Amazon's marketplace, incentivizing them to sell exclusively on it. Amazon Prime, which gives subscribers free two-day shipping on many products, helps the company reduce online shoppers' tendency to multi-home.

Network Bridging

In many situations the best growth strategy for a platform may be to connect different networks to one another. In any platform business, success hinges on acquiring a high number of users and amassing data on their interactions. Such assets can almost invariably be valuable in multiple scenarios and markets. By leveraging them, firms that have succeeded in one industry vertical often diversify into different lines of business and improve their economics. This is a fundamental reason why Amazon and Alibaba have moved into so many markets.

When platform owners connect with multiple networks, they can build important synergies. Alibaba successfully bridged its payment platform, Alipay, with its e-commerce platforms Taobao and Tmall, providing a much-needed service to both buyers and sellers and fostering trust between them. Alibaba has also taken advantage of transaction and user data from Taobao and Tmall to launch new offerings through its financial services arm, Ant Financial— including a credit-rating system for merchants and consumers. And information from that rating system allowed Ant Financial to issue short-term consumer and merchant loans with very low default rates. With those loans, consumers can purchase more products on Alibaba's e-commerce platforms, and Alibaba's merchants can fund more inventory. These networks mutually reinforce one another's market positions, helping each network sustain its scale. Indeed, even after the rival platform Tencent offered a competing digital wallet service, WeChat Pay, through its app WeChat, Alipay remained attractive to consumers and merchants because of its tight bridging with Alibaba and Ant Financial's other services.

As the most successful platforms connect across more and more markets, they're becoming increasingly effective at tying together industries. Just as the Alibaba Group moved from commerce to financial services, Amazon has moved beyond retail to entertainment and consumer electronics. Platforms are thus becoming crucial hubs in the global economy.

When evaluating an opportunity involving a platform, entrepreneurs (and investors) should analyze the basic properties of the networks it will use and consider ways to strengthen network effects. It's also critical to evaluate the feasibility of minimizing multi-homing, building global network structures, and using network bridging to increase scale while mitigating the risk of disintermediation. That exercise will illuminate the key challenges of growing and sustaining the platform and help businesspeople develop more-realistic assessments of the platform's potential to capture value.

As for Didi and Uber, our analysis doesn't hold out much hope. Their networks consist of many highly local clusters. They both face rampant multi-homing, which may worsen as more rivals enter the markets. Network-bridging opportunities—their best hope—so far have had only limited success. They've been able to establish bridges just with other highly competitive businesses, like food delivery and snack vending. (In 2018 Uber struck a deal to place Cargo's snack vending machines in its vehicles, for instance.) And the inevitable rise of self-driving taxis will probably make it challenging for Didi and Uber to sustain their market capitalization. Network properties are trumping platform scale.

Originally published in January–February 2019. Reprint R1901J

Spontaneous Deregulation

by Benjamin Edelman and Damien Geradin

MANY SUCCESSFUL PLATFORM BUSINESSES—think Airbnb, Uber, and YouTube—ignore laws and regulations that appear to preclude their approach. Caught up, perhaps, by enthusiasm for their model and a belief in its utility for customers, the founders and managers of these companies seem to see many of the existing rules as unwanted holdovers from a bygone era not yet ready for their innovations. In this worldview, the laws and regulations need to be changed to reflect new tech-enabled realities. Perhaps the rule breakers also remember the maxim credited to Grace Murray Hopper, a pioneering naval officer and computer programmer: It's easier to ask for forgiveness than to get permission.

This rule flouting is a phenomenon we call "spontaneous private deregulation," and it is not new. Innovation has often rendered laws and regulations obsolete. As the sidebar "Spontaneous Deregulation in an Earlier Era" explains, the budding automobile and aviation industries faced similar challenges. Of course, laws are often necessary and appropriate, and spontaneous deregulation can sometimes be problematic. Many people with disabilities can't use Uber or Lyft because those services do not have to guarantee wheelchair accessibility, unlike taxi fleet firms in most U.S. jurisdictions. And as one of us (Edelman) found in a recent study with Michael Luca and Daniel Svirsky, some customers in the Airbnb world are more equal than others. (See the sidebar "More Downsides to Deregulation.")

Benign or otherwise, spontaneous deregulation is happening increasingly rapidly and in ever more industries. A decade ago, new software start-ups like Napster and YouTube ushered in a wave of piracy that rendered copyright laws effectively irrelevant and drove media companies closer to the brink of failure. Today platforms such as Uber launch new transportation services with or without licenses, while Airbnb hosts skip the taxes, zoning, and safety protections that add complexity and expense to the hotel business. Other new platforms offer prepared foods without meeting the requirements that apply to restaurants regarding health inspections, food safety training, zoning, and taxation. As all these platforms reshape markets, the scope of activity subject to regulation tends to decrease, and various forms of protection disappear.

In this environment, managers in a range of industries need to assess the threat of spontaneous private deregulation. Forward-thinking leaders should plan their responses—an exercise bound to be challenging as they consider ignoring laws they have spent decades learning to follow.

You May Be More Vulnerable Than You Think

A striking variety of firms face potential threats from spontaneous private deregulation. For example, many lawyers perform services that don't really require the personal engagement of an expensive trained professional. Consider routine real estate transactions, uncontested divorces, and small-business contracts. (In fact, in most law firms these matters are already handled largely by paralegals, but at prices that include attorney overhead.) Similarly, investment bankers may become less important as web-based platforms enable entrepreneurs to sell equity directly to both individual and institutional investors.

In many situations the threat comes from innovators that find ways to leverage the underused capabilities or assets of private individuals, realizing both lower costs and greater flexibility. Previously, successful companies could satisfy customers by combining specialized equipment with staff trained and supervised in the use

Idea in Brief

The Problem

In more and more industries, innovative new platforms sidestep regulations that load costs onto incumbent players and restrict their ability to compete.

Why It Happens

Regulations may be excessive or obsolete, protecting consumers against low-probability risks. In such situations, the case for respecting the rules is weakened. Another factor is that the authorities may be slow to enforce regulations, leaving incumbents subject to rules that entrants avoid.

The Response

Incumbent firms have four options. They can take legal action to try to get the current laws enforced. Alternatively, they can embrace aspects of the new entrant's model or look for ways to leverage what they do best. As a last resort, incumbents may have little choice but to bow gracefully out of business.

of that equipment. But many private individuals also have assets—think cars and spare rooms—with excess capacity that can be profitably deployed through tech-enabled platforms like Uber and Airbnb. And such casual providers may not consider it a hardship to work nights and weekends, when established companies ordinarily need to pay premium wages. At the same time, many of the skills traditionally learned from employers can now be taught through software, supplemented when needed with training videos and other limited guidance. Finally, private individuals can more easily avoid regulations that constrain established commercial providers: For example, taxis have to wait in a queue at most airports, but Uber cars cut the line.

High-end incumbents often believe that they occupy a relatively safe niche, but they are threatened too. Black-car service may be superior to Uber because it allows customers to make advance reservations, but if you need a car on short notice, Uber probably has one in your area—perhaps even a luxury car. In the hotel industry, secure market positions are equally uncertain. Four Seasons might think it's in a different league from properties on Airbnb, but Airbnb now offers a remarkable array of deluxe options. In New York City alone, it has several hundred listings priced above $500 per night, including penthouse suites that easily match luxury hotel accommodations.

To figure out whether your industry and company are vulnerable, ask yourself the following questions.

Are Consumers Being Unnecessarily Protected?

Many industries require that providers be licensed to operate. In most cases these requirements are intended to safeguard consumers by providing some degree of quality assurance, even if they also end up shielding incumbents from competition. But many successful new platforms simply ignore the legal requirements. How do they get away with it? A common defense is to claim that consumers can dispense with traditional protections because the platform offers an alternative, possibly superior protection mechanism.

This mechanism is often an online reputation system. For example, passengers can rate Uber's drivers, and customers can check a driver's rating before accepting service. Meanwhile, drivers are operating their own vehicles and thus have a direct incentive to keep them in good condition. Furthermore, passengers might notice serious safety shortfalls and alert others through an unfavorable rating. Perhaps Uber's approach is imperfect, but licensing isn't necessarily more reassuring. After riding in a less-than-sparkling taxicab, a passenger can't help wondering what corners taxis might cut in vehicle maintenance as well as cleanliness. Combine the questionable effectiveness of government oversight with platforms' incentives for good performance, and it's arguable that compliance functions are best left to the likes of Uber, Airbnb, and their decentralized service providers, rather than to the government.

Formal regulation of many other service providers—from tax advisers to real estate agents to venture capitalists—may be equally unnecessary. The public's comfort in using unlicensed competitors depends on consumers' ability to detect substandard service and their willingness to bear the costs if the service disappoints. Few people would accept heart surgery from an unqualified practitioner, but the risk of an unsafe vehicle seems modest in most American cities. To be sure, serious problems have been reported with some Uber drivers and Airbnb hosts, including physical and sexual assaults, but dangers can also exist in taxis and hotels, and a thoughtful consumer would struggle to figure out where the risk is greatest.

With limited information, consumer beliefs and attitudes play an important role. An anxious first-time home buyer may be willing to pay for a lawyer to manage a title transfer in order to have peace of mind; an experienced property investor might prefer to save on the fees. Tired business travelers may want the comfort of knowing what to expect at check-in—a standard room and services, with someone ready to greet them no matter what time they arrive. However, a globe-trotting extrovert might relish the adventure of staying in a host's spare room.

If the need for protection is relatively low and customers can easily acquire any relevant knowledge, then the industry is vulnerable to a platform that pushes past regulation. The vulnerability is particularly acute if (as is often the case) the regulatory system has created an oligopoly, protecting license holders from price competition and the need to be responsive to certain customer concerns. Indeed, the success of Uber owes much to the fact that many cities restricted the number of taxi licenses, creating a shortage of vehicles and reducing the interest of license holders in investing to improve their service. That created an opening for Uber drivers, who have a personal stake in important aspects of quality because they drive their own cars, and who provide customers with easier access to rides at peak times because there are no controls on the supply of vehicles.

Can Your Business Practices Be Codified?

Incumbent firms typically have processes for assuring quality, most notably through the selection and training of employees. For example, hotel chains ensure that rooms are clean by training and supervising the housekeeping staff. In many cases, the law mandates that workers complete certain courses and demonstrate certain competencies. Most states, for instance, require real estate professionals to pass exams about the home-buying process and property regulations, and aspiring plumbers, electricians, cooks, and myriad other service providers must also satisfy state standards.

Of course, much of the knowledge involved in this training can be and is codified. As more people get access to this information, ordinary consumers are increasingly able to perform many of the routine practices that were previously reserved for regulated firms and specialists. This advance draws partly on a culture of self-help: Why call a registered plumber to fix your water purifier if you can watch a free online video and do it yourself—or have a handy friend take care of it for far less than the plumber would charge?

The threat of spontaneous deregulation is compounded when software platforms reduce the quality and reliability gap between casual providers and firms employing licensed professionals. London's famous black-cab taxi drivers previously boasted an unrivaled command of the city's geography; acquiring that in-depth knowledge required intensive training and examination. Now anyone with Google Maps can take you from Piccadilly to Putney. Similarly, some consumers and small businesses have found that tools like QuickBooks and TurboTax offer an attractive substitute for formal accounting training. Routine legal transactions are likewise becoming manageable without three years of law school, thanks to digital tools.

At the same time, online platforms make it easy to dispatch the growing number of semi-specialists who have a bit of experience albeit perhaps no official certification. Services that might formerly have seemed "marginal" increasingly seem "good enough." Thus to meet ordinary needs, specialized training may become difficult to justify, as software platforms deliver a phalanx of casual competitors with sufficient quality and a systematic cost advantage.

The more readily a business's methods can be codified, and the more readily its benefits can be provided by self-trained or tech-enabled enthusiasts, the more vulnerable that business is to low-cost competition from spontaneous private deregulation.

Do the Regulations Protect Third Parties?

Many regulations are imposed on businesses to ensure the welfare of other parties besides customers. Automobile safety requirements protect not just the people using the cars but also bystanders who might be injured by catastrophic failures. Power companies have to avoid excessive pollution not solely for the good of their customers but also because air quality affects everyone.

Typically, the cost of meeting regulations gets passed on to each firm's respective customers. But companies that are subject to those regulations are vulnerable to competition from platforms that facilitate less-accountable relationships. Often, when a platform coordinates hundreds or thousands of casual providers, it becomes unclear just who is harming the third parties or how existing rules apply to the web of relationships.

For example, a city may require special fire-safety equipment for commercial real estate and short-term rentals. Who is responsible for ensuring the installation of such equipment—Airbnb, its hosts, both, or neither? This ambiguity enables both parties to avoid investing in the fire-safety measures and to pass on their savings to customers via lower prices. Plenty of customers are happy to accept this trade-off, but third parties who might be affected by a fire aren't in a position to make the choice. And if some properties (such as those that brand themselves hotels) are rigorously inspected and others (Airbnb accommodations) are not, the former will find themselves at a cost disadvantage.

Crafting a Response

The businesses at greatest risk of spontaneous private deregulation are those that answer yes to all three questions: Are consumers being unnecessarily protected? Can business practices be codified? Are third parties being protected? Often regulators themselves worry that some rules may be excessive, or at least ineffective. When private individuals begin to provide services, they usually fly under the regulatory radar at first, making it especially easy for them to find

Spontaneous Deregulation in an Earlier Era

RAPID TECHNOLOGICAL CHANGE forces us to reevaluate which laws are still needed. That was as true decades ago as it is now.

Automobiles

At the dawn of mechanized transportation, the British Parliament's Locomotive Acts established onerous requirements for all mechanically propelled vehicles. In 1865, vehicles were limited to traveling two miles per hour in cities, towns, and villages, and four miles per hour elsewhere. Vehicle operators particularly disliked the requirement that three people attend the vehicle at all times, with one of them assigned to carry a red flag at least 60 yards ahead of it to warn approaching horseback riders and horse-drawn carriages.

A few drivers flouted the law, risking fines as large as £10 (equivalent to more than $1,100 in 2015). Over time, as more people became aware of the benefits of automobiles and as fears proved overblown, support for the Locomotive Acts waned, and the rules were significantly loosened in 1896.

Airplanes

Regulatory questions also arose at the dawn of aviation a few decades later. The Romans had held that a landowner's property extended "from the bowels of the earth to the heavens above." British and American law copied that approach. But in the 1900s, anyone piloting a plane would necessarily pass over thousands of parcels with diverse ownership. Aviation would collapse under the administrative burden of negotiating flying rights with every landowner. Fortunately Congress recognized the problem, and in 1940 it declared "navigable airspace" to be free for everyone to use, with no permission required from landowners below. Here, at least, legal rules imposed little real barrier to transportation innovation.

footholds. As they gain popularity, they may seem virtually unstoppable and even praiseworthy—all the more so when harmed parties, such as noncustomer third parties, have little ability or incentive to speak up.

An incumbent might consider acquiring a threatening entrant. But if the entrant's value grows as rapidly as we have seen with

Airbnb and Uber, this quickly becomes unrealistic. And incumbents could hardly claim the regulatory high ground if their response to allegedly illegal entry was to acquire the entrant and embrace the same methods.

So let's turn now to the strategic options that are open to businesses at risk of experiencing spontaneous private deregulation—or already facing the threat.

Option 1: Call Your Lawyer

When a competitor enters the market and ignores key regulations, it is natural to seek legal assistance—perhaps through private litigation or by urging a regulator to take action. When violations are clear-cut, this strategy can be effective, if the incumbents and those protected by the regulations unite behind it. For example, in 1999, copyright holders began to sue software companies that were facilitating copyright infringement, and their litigation successes compelled the shutdown of Napster's file-sharing service (among others).

Yet this strategy has important limitations. Legal action can be slow, costly, and unpredictable. Moreover, courts often take a dim view of competitors seeking to enforce regulations, finding that only regulators have the authority to do so. More than a dozen taxi associations, fleet owners, and operators have sued Uber in the United States, but almost all the cases have been dismissed as invalid on procedural grounds. Uber's critics have had more success outside the United States, especially in Western Europe, but some people have attributed the rulings against Uber to anti-American sentiment and to incumbents' co-opting of the regulators. On the whole, Uber's approach has prevailed in most regions worldwide.

There is another key drawback to filing suit. Legal action assumes that laws will remain as they are. But if consumers embrace an entrant's approach, laws may change—sometimes rapidly. Upstarts have discovered the power of mobilizing their users to influence regulators. For example, Uber has encouraged its passengers to contact regulators in cities where its service has been banned or is at risk of being banned. In contrast, an incumbent usually lacks popular support when seeking to maintain the status quo. Any lawsuit is vulnerable to ever-shifting political debates, which in turn influence legal requirements. An incumbent who sues may look like a sore loser in the public's eye—and may be a loser in court as well, if legal rules shift or an unsympathetic legal system undermines the suit.

Option 2: Embrace Aspects of the New Model

For an incumbent facing a creative entrant, a natural starting point is to adopt the best aspects of the competitor's approach. This is a promising way to neutralize new rivals and remain viable. For example, Napster came on the scene with music that was usually copyright-infringing, but the service's real value lay in its ability to provide songs nearly instantly to any device. In contrast, early online music sales platforms asked users to navigate a multistep purchase process and then delivered files encrypted with digital rights management (DRM) technology. This meant the files could be played only on a limited set of compatible devices, and the music was often difficult to transfer if a consumer changed devices.

Of course, music sellers had every reason to fear piracy. But locking their content behind DRM probably pushed consumers into piracy more than it increased sales. Facing competition from copyright infringement and pressure from e-retailers, music sellers ultimately embraced unencrypted files that widened consumers' options. Legal music sales might have taken off faster, and piracy might have been correspondingly reduced, had rights holders recognized that Napster owed its success as much to its convenience as to the fact that it was free.

Similarly, Uber and Lyft attracted customers with user-friendly platforms providing quick and reliable service. Customers also relished the opportunity to rate drivers, yielding incentives for safe and polite service. To stay in the game, taxi operators in most cities launched their own applications and made efforts to improve service quality. Many passengers think arranging a cab ride means

More Downsides to Deregulation

SPONTANEOUS PRIVATE DEREGULATION tends to give consumers more choices. But it's difficult to celebrate some other effects.

Discrimination

Laws (at least in the United States) require equal treatment of all guests, regardless of race, who book at hotel websites or through travel agents. But it is unclear whether or how this requirement applies to less-regulated platforms like Airbnb. In a field experiment, one of us (Edelman, with Mike Luca and Dan Svirsky) found that Airbnb hosts were 16% less likely to accept a reservation request if the guest's name suggested black rather than white ethnicity. (All requests were fictitious; the team created identical profiles for would-be guests but attached names that census records and survey data showed were disproportionately associated with particular races.)

Tax Avoidance

Commercial vehicles usually pay higher fees for registration, tolls, and the like than do the owners of private cars participating in platforms such as Uber. Similarly, hotel rooms tend to be highly taxed, whereas rooms booked through Airbnb and other platforms usually go untaxed. Governments need revenue, and it's hard to see why some providers should contribute while others are exempt. That said, modern platforms create an electronic record of every transaction, facilitating tax collection in sectors like taxis, where cash payments previously invited tax evasion.

---

a phone call to a grumpy dispatcher, but taxi companies now widely offer web- and app-based ordering, through a customer interface not unlike Uber's (in fact, some taxi fleets offered web-based booking years before Uber). Even vehicle-en-route tracking has been around for years. If a taxi fleet operator complains about Uber but fails to offer these services, it's hard to feel much sympathy.

Nonetheless, copying the entrant's strategy can be tough to put into practice. For one thing, most incumbents build up capabilities that are not useful in the new entrants' models. Consider the skills required to run a national hotel chain—attracting and supervising franchisees, coordinating marketing efforts, booking conferences and events. It's unlikely that these skills translate to success in a world where short-term accommodations follow Airbnb's model. In fact, staff trained in the old way may resist the changes, or at least struggle to implement them.

Moreover, incomplete efforts to adopt a new model may be tragically ineffective. Consider a taxi fleet operator concerned about competition from app-based transportation services. Uber claims important cost advantages: It doesn't buy medallions (operating licenses), forgoes commercial vehicle registration and insurance, and sidesteps the driver verification that many cities require of taxis. Woe to the fleet operator who expects an online booking feature to overcome that cost gap. When Hailo tried to organize New York taxis via a modern app, its prices were always higher than Uber's—predictably disappointing the customers concerned about the cost of a ride.

Option 3: Play to Your Strengths

New platforms typically offer some benefits, but there are usually also downsides. Novice Uber drivers, for example, won't know shortcuts commonly used by experienced taxi drivers. And an Airbnb stay may give travelers an "authentic" taste of the local culture, but if a delayed flight complicates meeting the host, the guest will surely miss the convenience of a front desk open around the clock. Incumbents should remind consumers of the advantages they offer; for the right customers in the right circumstances, the message may resonate.

For example, forward-thinking hotel operators are playing to their strengths as they adjust their offerings in the face of competition from Airbnb. New "pod"-style hotels forgo oversized guest rooms and deluxe furniture. Yet by gathering a group of travelers in a single building with comfortable common areas, they create social environments that scattered Airbnb properties can't match. And with smaller rooms and basic fixtures, their costs may approach or even beat those of informal competitors. CitizenM, the Pod Hotel, and Yotel are testing this model in New York City and several cities in Europe, and it seems to be gaining traction.

A big challenge for many incumbents is that when customers assess available options, they often pay no attention to the potential for unanticipated problems. To be sure, the consequences of not having a fire escape in your Airbnb room or being driven by a bad Uber driver can be severe—indeed, deadly. But rare is the consumer who actually considers the probabilities, let alone the possibilities. Perhaps a safer room or a professional driver transforms a one-in-10-million risk into one in 20 million. At $20 extra, is that a good deal? Most of us could run the analysis if the numbers were known, but these risks tend to be uncertain and difficult to measure.

Option 4: Bow to the Inevitable

Google's widely used YouTube video service began as a classic example of spontaneous private deregulation. It hosted copyright-infringing videos uploaded by the service's users (and sometimes by its founders). Fast-forward a few years, and record company executives found themselves up against a wall in their negotiations with YouTube. They ultimately accepted modest royalties because the only apparent alternative was piracy, which paid them nothing at all. No one faults them for choosing the former, but it was a painful outcome for record companies, as it left them with a small fraction of their prior revenue. Their experience illustrates the potential for losses when firms are too slow to respond to changing conditions, both in law and in practice.

Still, if spontaneous private deregulation is unavoidable and the prior options offer little promise, the best response may well be an early, voluntary dissolution, expensive as that can be. If you were holding taxi medallions, for example, you might prefer to sell them and cut your losses, accepting a price well below the recent peak, because the alternative could be still worse. Indeed, several taxi fleets attributed their recent bankruptcies to competition from Uber. Ceasing operation is obviously not an incumbent's preferred strategy; it's far better for threatened companies to address their vulnerabilities early on. But accepting and planning for the inevitable may be the best and least expensive response in an industry whose changing norms and sources of competitive advantage have made a company's assets and capabilities largely redundant.

Looking Forward

While incumbents often find it tempting to accuse platform-based companies of unfair play, there is little doubt that these platforms are here to stay—and grow. Technological innovation makes it possible for software applications to carry out increasingly complex tasks, and two-sided platforms that connect casual providers with customers are well-positioned to leapfrog traditional firms. To survive, incumbents in industries that are vulnerable to software platforms must themselves adopt modern tools but also play to their strengths. In many ways, Uber and Airbnb seduced consumers who were disenchanted with the services provided by taxicabs and hotel chains. With diligence and foresight, other established providers can avoid a similar loss of customers.

Originally published in April 2016. Reprint R1604F

How Online Marketplaces Can Effectively Navigate Regulatory Risk

by Andrei Hagiu and Simon Rothman

Online marketplaces that provide radically new alternatives to conventional business models test the limits of existing regulatory frameworks almost by definition. They enable new types of transactions, such as peer-to-peer lending or property rentals. As a result, marketplaces face serious regulatory challenges much more frequently than traditional product or service companies do. Should homeowners renting out their properties be subject to hotel taxes?

Under what conditions should individuals be allowed to sell rides in their cars? When should marketplaces for services be allowed to treat their service providers as independent contractors and when should they be compelled to treat them as employees?

With respect to regulatory risks, most entrepreneurs have one of two reflexes: ignore them or try to fix everything up front. Neither is a good idea. Unwinding a regulatory problem late tends to be much more difficult than preventing it early. Furthermore, ignoring regulations can generate bad press, which may alienate users. At the other extreme, attempting to clear all regulatory hurdles from the beginning is unrealistic. Regulatory time frames are too long for most young companies to work within, and it is very hard to gain clearance for a business concept that has not yet been proved in the market.

The right approach, not surprisingly, is somewhere in the middle: Strive to engage regulators without breaking stride or slowing down to the decision-making speed of governments. No marketplace we know of has dealt with all its regulatory challenges perfectly, but four interconnected guiding principles—developed by David Hantman, Airbnb's former head of global public policy—can help.

1. Define Yourself before Your Opposition or the Media Does

Marketplace entrepreneurs should develop a clear vision of their business model and find the most positive—yet accurate—way to describe it to the outside world. Then they should engage regulators and the media to ensure that they are understood on their own terms.

2. Pick the Time and Place to Engage with Regulators

Entrepreneurs operating in industries subject to heavy and national regulation should consult an industry attorney before launch in order to fully understand all relevant laws. As soon as their buyer-seller proposition is clear, they should initiate a dialogue with regulators in order to obtain either explicit legal clearance (ideal) or an implicit safe haven (second best) for continuing to develop the service.

The examples of Lending Club and Prosper, the two leading peer-to-peer lending marketplaces in the United States, illustrate the importance of smoothing regulatory frictions before they grind you to a halt. Prosper was launched first, in 2005, followed by Lending Club a year later. Lending Club, however, was first to tackle the difficult regulatory issues. Less than two years after its launch, it established a partnership with an FDIC-insured bank so that the loans it facilitated were subject to the same borrower protection, fair lending, and disclosure regulations as regular bank loans. In early 2008, it became the first peer-to-peer lending marketplace to voluntarily go through a quiet period during which it did not accept any new lenders and focused on completing its registration with the U.S. Securities and Exchange Commission (SEC) as an issuer of public investment products.

In contrast, Prosper ignored regulatory issues until scrutiny by the SEC forced it, too, to enter a quiet period. The results of these differing approaches were significant: Prosper's quiet period lasted nine months, whereas Lending Club's lasted just six. And Lending Club was allowed to continue to serve the borrower side of its marketplace during its quiet period; Prosper had to shut down both the investor and the borrower sides. Lending Club eventually overtook Prosper to become the largest peer-to-peer lending marketplace: In 2012, it made $718 million in loans, compared with $153 million for Prosper.

At the other end of the spectrum, marketplaces operating in spaces that are regulated lightly and only at the city or state level can afford to wait until they reach supply-demand fit in their first city before engaging with regulators. While regulatory issues at the national level are usually a matter of life and death for companies, local regulators are typically less powerful and can be more easily circumvented if necessary.

3. Don't Just Say No; Offer Constructive Ideas

When confronted with regulatory gray areas—an all-too-common occurrence—marketplace entrepreneurs have an opportunity to turn a potentially adversarial relationship with regulators into a partnership. For example, Getaround, the peer-to-peer car rental platform, preempted a collision by working directly with the California state government to enact a law that allows private individuals to rent out their cars to strangers under separate insurance coverage designed for this purpose. Getaround's approach is remarkable because peer-to-peer car rentals were not explicitly illegal beforehand—meaning that the company incurred a significant risk by drawing regulatory attention to its service.

Even when existing regulations are merely inconvenient for new marketplaces, entrepreneurs should resist the temptation to ignore or thumb their noses at the relevant authorities and strive instead to find an area where their interests align. For example, a major concern for governmental bodies that regulate taxis is ensuring the safety of passengers and drivers. Ride-sharing companies should want the same thing. The marketplaces could use their data on driver and passenger identity and on trip times and paths to work constructively with state regulators to create a safer environment than traditional taxi companies provide.

4. Speak Softly and Carry a Big Stick

Entrepreneurs should avoid engaging in acrimonious disputes with regulators; at the same time, they should have effective weapons at their disposal to defend their position. They can use two means of leverage when fighting potentially adverse regulation. The first is the power of satisfied buyers and sellers, who are voters and taxpayers likely to resent government interference with a service they value. To harness the support of users, companies should develop a credible infrastructure for running lobbying campaigns in their own behalf: social media, dedicated websites, and so on. For example, Airbnb helped its San Francisco hosts organize rallies around city hall and testify in public hearings, which eventually swayed the city's regulators to legalize short-term rentals in people's homes in 2014 (the "Airbnb law").

The second lever is tax revenue. Marketplaces that generate sizable revenues for local governments have some leverage in regulatory negotiations. For instance, as part of its ongoing efforts to persuade city governments to legalize its service, Airbnb has offered to collect hotel taxes from its hosts and remit them to local authorities in several cities worldwide. This offer, still pending approval, is clearly a powerful negotiating instrument: According to conservative estimates, the taxable revenue generated by Airbnb hosts was more than $5 billion in 2015. This is an interesting case, since few marketplaces have proactively offered to take responsibility for ensuring that their users pay taxes.

Sometimes, if regulatory uncertainty is unlikely to be resolved in the immediate future (a time frame measured in months for start-ups) and the repercussions of noncompliance are severe, then the right response is to comply with the worst-case scenario, even if that means incurring higher costs. One of the most serious regulatory issues now faced by service marketplaces concerns the legal status of their workers. Several prominent service marketplaces (Handy, Lyft, Postmates, Uber, and Washio) are currently contending with class-action lawsuits that accuse them of improperly classifying their workers as independent contractors rather than employees. The cost implications are substantial: Changing a worker's status from independent contractor to employee increases costs by 25% to 40%. While the outcomes of the lawsuits and the corresponding regulation are still uncertain, some marketplace start-ups, including Alfred, Enjoy Technology, Luxe, and Managed by Q, have preempted the issue by voluntarily turning their workers into employees. Early stage start-ups that simply cannot afford to operate under uncertain regulatory status may need to do the same. In most cases, however, an intermediate status somewhere between employee and independent contractor would be the ideal approach.

Adapted from content originally published in April 2016. Reprint R1604D.

Alibaba and the Future of Business

by Ming Zeng

ALIBABA HIT THE HEADLINES with the world's biggest IPO in September 2014. Today, the company has a market cap among the global top 10, has surpassed Walmart in global sales, and has expanded into all the major markets in the world. Founder Jack Ma has become a household name.

From its inception, in 1999, Alibaba experienced great growth on its e-commerce platform. However, it still didn't look like a world-beater in 2007 when the management team, which I had joined full-time the year before, met for a strategy off-site at a drab seaside hotel in Ningbo, Zhejiang province. Over the course of the meeting, our disjointed observations and ideas about e-commerce trends began to coalesce into a larger view of the future, and by the end, we had agreed on a vision. We would "foster the development of an open, coordinated, prosperous e- commerce ecosystem." That's when Alibaba's journey really began.

Alibaba's special innovation, we realized, was that we were truly building an ecosystem: a community of organisms (businesses and consumers of many types) interacting with one another and the environment (the online platform and the larger off-line physical elements). Our strategic imperative was to make sure that the platform provided all the resources, or access to the resources, that an online business would need to succeed, and hence supported the evolution of the ecosystem.

The ecosystem we built was simple at first: We linked buyers and sellers of goods. As technology advanced, more business functions moved online—including established ones, such as advertising, marketing, logistics, and finance, and emerging ones, such as affiliate marketing, product recommenders, and social media influencers. And as we expanded our ecosystem to accommodate these innovations, we helped create new types of online businesses, completely reinventing China's retail sector along the way.

Alibaba today is not just an online commerce company. It is what you get if you take all functions associated with retail and coordinate them online into a sprawling, data-driven network of sellers, marketers, service providers, logistics companies, and manufacturers. In other words, Alibaba does what Amazon, eBay, PayPal, Google, FedEx, wholesalers, and a good portion of manufacturers do in the United States, with a healthy helping of financial services for garnish.

Of the world's 10 most highly valued companies today, seven are internet companies with business models similar to ours. Five of them—Amazon, Google, and Facebook in the United States and Alibaba and Tencent in China—have been around barely 20 years. Why has so much value and market power emerged so quickly? Because of new capabilities in network coordination and data intelligence that all these companies put to use. The ecosystems they steward are vastly more economically efficient and customer-centric than traditional industries. These firms follow an approach I call smart business, and I believe it represents the dominant business logic of the future.

What Is Smart Business?

Smart business emerges when all players involved in achieving a common business goal—retailing, for example, or ride sharing—are coordinated in an online network and use machine-learning technology to efficiently leverage data in real time. This tech-enabled model, in which most operational decisions are made by machines, allows companies to adapt dynamically and rapidly to changing

Idea in Brief

A New Business Model

Alibaba is an example of tomorrow's "smart business": a tech-enabled platform that coordinates multiple business players in an ecosystem.

How It Works

Players in the ecosystem share data and apply machine-learning technology to identify and better fulfill consumer needs.

How to Build It

Automate decision making by:

- making sure every interaction yields as much data as possible

- ensuring that all business activities are mediated by software

- using APIs and other interface protocols to ensure smooth interaction among software systems

- applying machine learning to make sense of data in real time

market conditions and customer preferences, gaining tremendous competitive advantage over traditional businesses.

Ample computing power and digital data are the fuel for machine learning, of course. The more data and the more iterations the algorithmic engine goes through, the better its output gets. Data scientists come up with probabilistic prediction models for specific actions, and then the algorithm churns through loads of data to produce better decisions in real time with every iteration. These prediction models become the basis for most business decisions. Thus machine learning is more than a technological innovation; it will transform the way business is conducted as human decision making is increasingly replaced by algorithmic output.

Ant Microloans provides a striking example of what this future will look like. When Alibaba launched Ant, in 2012, the typical loan given by large banks in China was in the millions of dollars. The minimum loan amount—about 6 million RMB or just under $1 million—was well above the amounts needed by most small and medium-size enterprises (SMEs). Banks were reluctant to service companies that lacked any kind of credit history or even adequate documentation of their business activities. As a consequence, tens of millions of businesses in China were having real difficulties securing the money necessary to grow their operations.

At Alibaba, we realized we had the ingredient for creating a high-functioning, scalable, and profitable SME lending business: the huge amount of transaction data generated by the many small businesses using our platform. So in 2010 we launched a pioneering data-driven microloan business to offer loans to businesses in amounts no larger than 1 million RMB (about $160,000). In seven years of operation, the business has lent more than 87 billion RMB ($13.4 billion) to nearly three million SMEs. The average loan size is 8,000 RMB, or about $1,200. In 2012, we bundled this lending operation together with Alipay, our very successful payments business, to create Ant Financial Services. We gave the new venture that name to capture the idea that we were empowering all the little but industrious, ant-like companies.

Today, Ant can easily process loans as small as several hundred RMB (around $50) in a few minutes. How is this possible? When faced with potential borrowers, lending institutions need answer only three basic questions: Should we lend to them, how much should we lend, and at what interest rate? Once sellers on our platforms gave us authorization to analyze their data, we were well positioned to answer those questions. Our algorithms can look at transaction data to assess how well a business is doing, how competitive its offerings are in the market, whether its partners have high credit ratings, and so on.

Ant uses that data to compare good borrowers (those who repay on time) with bad ones (those who do not) to isolate traits common in both groups. Those traits are then used to calculate credit scores. All lending institutions do this in some fashion, of course, but at Ant the analysis is done automatically on all borrowers and on all their behavioral data in real time. Every transaction, every communication between seller and buyer, every connection with other services available at Alibaba, indeed every action taken on our platform, affects a business's credit score. At the same time, the algorithms that calculate the scores are themselves evolving in real time, improving the quality of decision making with each iteration.

Determining how much to lend and how much interest to charge requires analysis of many types of data generated inside the Alibaba network, such as gross profit margins and inventory turnover, along with less mathematically precise information such as product life cycles and the quality of a seller's social and business relationships. The algorithms might, for example, analyze the frequency, length, and type of communications (instant messaging, e-mail, or other methods common in China) to assess relationship quality.

Alibaba's data scientists are essential in identifying and testing which data points provide the insights they seek and then engineering algorithms to mine the data. This work requires both a deep understanding of the business and expertise in machine-learning algorithms. Consider again Ant Financial. If a seller deemed to have poor credit pays back its loan on time or a seller with excellent credit catastrophically defaults, the algorithm clearly needs tweaking. Engineers can quickly and easily check their assumptions. Which parameters should be added or removed? Which kinds of user behavior should be given more weight?

As the recalibrated algorithms produce increasingly accurate predictions, Ant's risk and costs steadily decrease, and borrowers get the money they need, when they need it, at an interest rate they can afford. The result is a highly successful business: The microlending operation has a default rate of about 1%, far below the World Bank's 2016 estimate of an average of 4% worldwide.

So how do you create that kind of business?

Automate All Operating Decisions

To become a smart business, your firm must enable as many operating decisions as possible to be made by machines fueled by live data rather than by humans supported by their own data analysis. Transforming decision making in this way is a four-step process.

Step 1: "Datafy" every customer exchange
Ant was fortunate to have access to plenty of data on potential borrowers to answer the questions inherent in its lending business. For

Alibaba's Major Businesses at a Glance

Chinese Retail Marketplaces

Taobao Marketplace

Tmall

Rural Taobao

Cross-Border and Global Marketplaces

AliExpress

Tmall Global

Lazada

Wholesale Commerce

1688.com (China)

Alibaba.com (global)

Digital Media and Entertainment*

Youku Tudou (online video)

Alibaba Pictures

Alibaba Music

Alibaba Sports

UC (mobile browser)

Other Services*

AutoNavi (mapping and navigation)

Koubei (local services)

Ele.me (delivery)

Finance*

Ant Financial (includes Alipay)

MYbank

Logistics*

Cainiao Network

Cloud Computing*

Alibaba Cloud

* Major investee companies and cooperative partners of Alibaba Group

---

many businesses, the data capture process will be more challenging. But live data is essential to creating the feedback loops that are the basis of machine learning.

Consider the bike rental business. Start-ups in China have leveraged mobile telephony, the internet of things (in the form of smart bike locks), and existing mobile payment and credit systems to datafy the entire rental process.

Renting a bike traditionally involved going to a rental location, leaving a deposit, having someone give you a bike, using the bike, returning it, and then paying for the rental by cash or credit card. Several rival Chinese companies put all of this online by integrating various new technologies with existing ones. A crucial innovation was the combination of QR codes and electronic locks that cleverly automated the checkout process. By opening the bike-sharing app, a rider can see available bicycles and reserve one nearby. Once the rider arrives at the bicycle, he or she uses the app to scan a QR code on the bicycle. Assuming that the person has money in his or her account and meets the rental criteria, the QR code will open the electronic bike lock. The app can even verify the person's credit history through Sesame Credit, Ant Financial's new online product for consumer credit ratings, allowing the rider to skip paying a deposit, further expediting the process. When the bike is returned, closing the lock completes the transaction. The process is simple, intuitive, and usually takes only several seconds.

Datafying the rental process greatly improves the consumer experience. On the basis of live data, companies dispatch trucks to move bikes to where users want them. They can also alert regular users to the availability of bikes nearby. Thanks in large part to these innovations, the cost of bike rentals in China has fallen to just a few cents per hour.

Most businesses that seek to be more data-driven typically collect and analyze information in order to create a causal model. The model then isolates the critical data points from the mass of information available. That is not how smart businesses use data. Instead, they capture all information generated during exchanges and communications with customers and other network members as the business operates and then let the algorithms figure out what data is relevant.

Step 2: "Software" every activity
In a smart business, all activities—not just knowledge management and customer relations—are configured using software so that decisions affecting them can be automated. This does not mean that a firm needs to buy or build ERP software or its equivalent to manage its business—quite the opposite. Traditional software makes

processes and decision flows more rigid and often becomes a strait-jacket. In contrast, the dominant logic for smart business is reactivity in real time. The first step is to build a model of how humans currently make decisions and find ways to replicate the simpler elements of that process using software—which is not always easy, given that many human decisions are built on common sense or even subconscious neurological activity.

The growth of Taobao, the domestic retailing website of Alibaba Group, is driven by continuous softwaring of the retailing process. One of the first major software tools built on Taobao was an instant message tool called Wangwang, through which buyers and sellers can talk to each other easily. Using the tool, the sellers greet buyers, introduce products, negotiate prices, and so on, just as people do in a traditional retail shop. Alibaba also developed a set of software tools that help sellers design and launch a variety of sophisticated online shop fronts. Once online shops are up and running, sellers can access other software products to issue coupons, offer discounts, run loyalty programs, and conduct other customer relationship activities, all of which are coordinated with one another.

Because most software today is run online as a service, an important advantage of softwaring a business activity is that live data can be collected naturally as part of the business process, building the foundation for the application of machine-learning technologies.

Step 3: Get data flowing
In ecosystems with many interconnected players, business decisions require complex coordination. Taobao's recommendation engines, for example, need to work with the inventory management systems of sellers and with the consumer-profiling systems of various social media platforms. Its transaction systems need to work with discount offers and loyalty programs, as well as feed into our logistics network.

Communication standards, such as TCP/IP, and application programming interfaces (APIs) are critical in getting the data flowing among multiple players while ensuring strict control of who can access and edit data throughout the ecosystem. APIs, a set of tools that allow different software systems to "talk" and coordinate with one another online, have been central to Taobao's development. As the platform grew from a forum where buyers and sellers could meet and sell goods to become China's dominant e-commerce website, merchants on the site needed more and more support from third-party developers. New software had to be broadly interoperable with all other software on the platform to be of any value. So in 2009, Taobao began developing APIs for use by independent software suppliers. Today, merchants on Taobao subscribe to more than 100 software modules, on average, and the live data services they enable drastically decrease the merchants' cost of doing business.

Getting the technical infrastructure right is just the beginning. It took tremendous effort for us to build a common standard so that data could be used and interpreted in the same way across all of Alibaba's business units. Additionally, figuring out the right incentive structures to persuade companies to share the data they have is an important and ongoing challenge. Much more work is needed. Of course, the degree to which companies can innovate in this area will depend in part on the rules governing data sharing in the countries they're operating in. But the direction is very clear: The more data flows across the network, the smarter the business becomes, and the more value the ecosystem creates.

Step 4: Apply the algorithms

Once a business has all its operations online, it will experience a deluge of data. To assimilate, interpret, and use the data to its advantage, the firm must create models and algorithms that make explicit the underlying product logic or market dynamics that the business is trying to optimize. This is a huge creative undertaking that requires many new skills, hence the enormous demand for data scientists and economists. Their challenge is to specify what job they want the machine to do, and they have to be very clear about what constitutes a job well done in a particular business setting.

From very early on, our goal for Taobao was to tailor it to each individual's needs. This would have been impossible without advances in machine learning. Today, when customers log on, they see a customized webpage with a selection of products curated from the billions offered by our millions of sellers. The selection is generated automatically by Taobao's powerful recommendation engine. Its algorithms, which are designed to optimize the conversion rate of each visit, churn data generated across Taobao's platform, from operations to customer service to security.

A milestone in Taobao's growth, in 2009, was the upgrade from simple browsing, which worked reasonably well when the platform had many fewer visits and products to handle, to a search engine powered by machine-learning algorithms and capable of processing huge volumes of inquiries. Taobao has also been experimenting with optical-recognition search algorithms that can take a photo of a desired item supplied by the customer and match it to available products on the platform. While we are still in the early stages of using this technology to drive sales, the function has proved very popular with customers, boasting 10 million unique visits daily.

In 2016, Alibaba introduced an AI-powered chatbot to help field customer queries. It is different from the mechanical service providers familiar to most people that are programmed to match customer queries with answers in their repertoire. Alibaba's chatbots are "trained" by experienced representatives of Taobao merchants. They know all about the products in their categories and are well versed in the mechanics of Alibaba's platforms—return policies, delivery costs, how to make changes to an order—and other common questions customers ask. Using a variety of machine-learning technologies, such as semantic comprehension, context dialogues, knowledge graphs, data mining, and deep learning, the chatbots rapidly improve their ability to diagnose and fix customer issues automatically, rather than simply return static responses that prompt the consumer to take further action. They confirm with the customer that the solution presented is acceptable and then execute it. No human action by Alibaba or the merchant occurs.

Chatbots can also make a significant contribution to a seller's top line. Apparel brand Senma, for example, started using one a year ago and found that the bot's sales were 26 times higher than the merchant's top human sales associate.

There will always be a need for human customer representatives to deal with complicated or personal issues, but the ability to handle routine queries via a chatbot is very useful, especially on days of high volume or special promotions. Previously, most large sellers on our platform would hire temp workers to handle consumer inquiries during big events. Not anymore. During Alibaba's biggest sales day in 2017, the chatbot handled more than 95% of customer questions, responding to some 3.5 million consumers.

These four steps are the basis for creating a smart business: Engage in creative datafication to enrich the pool of data the business uses to become smarter; software the business to put workflows and essential actors online; institute standards and APIs to enable real-time data flow and coordination; and apply machine-learning algorithms to generate "smart" business decisions. All the activities involved in the four steps are important new competencies that require a new kind of leadership.

The Leader's Role

In my course on smart business at Hupan School of Entrepreneurship, I show a slide of 10 business leaders and ask the students to identify them. They can easily pick out Jack Ma, Elon Musk, and Steve Jobs. But virtually no one can identify the CEO of CitiGroup or Toyota or General Electric.

There is a reason for this. Unlike GE, Toyota, and CitiGroup, which deliver products or services through optimized supply chains, digital companies must mobilize a network to realize their vision. To do that, their leaders have to inspire the employees, partners, and customers who make up that network. They must be visionaries and evangelists, outspoken in a way that the leaders of traditional companies do not have to be.

At the highest level, the digital evangelists must understand what the future will look like and how their industries will evolve in response to societal, economic, and technological changes. They cannot describe concrete steps to realize their companies' goals because the environment is too fluid and the capabilities they will require are unknowable. Instead, they must define what the firm seeks to achieve and create an environment in which workers can quickly string together experimental products and services, test the market, and scale the ideas that elicit a positive response. Digital leaders no longer manage; rather, they enable workers to innovate and facilitate the core feedback loop of user responses to firm decisions and execution.

In the smart business model, machine-learning algorithms take on much of the burden of incremental improvement by automatically making adjustments that increase systemwide efficiency. Thus, leaders' most important job is to cultivate creativity. Their mandate is to increase the success rate of innovation rather than improve the efficiency of the operation.

Digital-native companies such as Alibaba have the advantage of being born online and data-ready, so their transformation to smart business is quite natural. Now that they have proven the model works and are transforming the old industrial economy, it is time for all companies to understand and apply this new business logic. That may look technologically intimidating, but it is becoming more and more feasible. The commercialization of cloud computing and artificial intelligence technologies has made large-scale computational power and analytic capabilities accessible to anyone. Indeed, the cost of storing and computing large quantities of data has dropped dramatically over the past decade. This means that real-time applications of machine learning are now possible and affordable in more and more environments. The rapid development of internet-of-things technology will further digitize our physical surroundings, providing ever more data. As these innovations accumulate in the coming decades, the winners will be companies that get smart faster than the competition.

Originally published in September–October 2018. Reprint R1805F

Fixing Discrimination in Online Marketplaces

by Ray Fisman and Michael Luca

IN THE LATE 1980S, law professors Ian Ayres and Peter Siegelman set out to learn whether blacks and women got the same deals as white men when buying a new car. They trained 38 people—some white and some black, some male and some female—to negotiate a purchase using a fixed script, and uncovered disturbing differences: across 153 dealerships, black and female buyers paid more for the same cars than white men did, with black women paying the most—on average, nearly $900 more than white men. Although the findings weren't a surprise to most people, least of all to blacks and women, they were a compelling demonstration of just how discriminatory markets can be.

Fast-forward a dozen years to the early days of internet commerce. Entrepreneurs were experimenting with web-based sales of everything, including automobiles. Economists Fiona Scott Morton, Florian Zettelmeyer, and Jorge Silva-Risso analyzed this new mode of selling cars and found that it did away with the racial and gender discrimination that, they also found, persisted in off-line automobile sales.

Indeed, the first generation of online marketplaces, including eBay, Amazon, and Priceline, made it hard for sellers to discriminate. Transactions were conducted with relative anonymity. A user could negotiate a purchase without providing any identifying information until the seller had agreed to the deal. As a *New Yorker* cartoon famously put it, "On the Internet, nobody knows you're a dog."

Except that platforms—and now their users—do know whether you're black or white, male or female, human or canine. And the internet has recently been revealed as a source of discrimination, not an end to it: With their identities uncovered, disadvantaged groups face many of the same challenges they have long confronted in the off-line world, sometimes made worse by a lack of regulation, the salience photos give to race and gender, and the fact that would-be discriminators can act without ever personally confronting their victims.

What happened, and what can we do about it?

The Emergence of Digital Discrimination

In the early days of e-commerce, shopping online often required a leap of faith. An eBay seller in Florida might post, say, a Topps baseball card for Nolan Ryan's 1974 season with the California Angels, along with a description of its condition. A collector in Massachusetts could bid on the card sight unseen, on the basis of that description. A card in mint condition might be valued at $60, but a dog-eared one would be worth just a fraction of that. What was to prevent the seller from passing off a well-worn card as pristine? Very little: A study by economists Ginger Jin and Andrew Kato found that in the early 2000s, eBay merchants often misrepresented the quality of sports trading cards.

The problem with early e-commerce was that one side of the market tended to know things the other side didn't—the condition of a baseball card, the reliability and care with which goods would be packaged, and so on. These challenges arise in all markets, but they were particularly severe for online platforms, for two main reasons. First, it's harder to overcome information asymmetries when you can't hold a product in your hand. Second, online sellers were, almost by definition, new to the business, since the business itself had been around for just a few years. There were no established brands, such as Sotheby's and Sears, to assure buyers they wouldn't be cheated.

Over time, buyer reviews and other feedback have allowed e-commerce sellers to build up reputations. But why stop at

Idea in Brief

The Problem

Online marketplaces such as eBay, Uber, and Airbnb have the potential to reduce racial, gender, and other kinds of discrimination that affect transactions in the off-line world. But recent research shows that the opposite has occurred.

The Reason

Early platforms kept the identities of buyers and sellers relatively anonymous. But the addition of photos, names, and other means of identification to listings has inadvertently encouraged discriminatory behavior.

The Answer

To create markets that are both efficient and inclusive, platform designers need to be mindful of the potential for discrimination and open to experimentation as they make choices about automation, algorithms, and the use of identifying data.

collecting feedback when so much potentially useful information could be mined from buyers' and sellers' identities? For example, in a 2012 study of peer-to-peer lending by Jefferson Duarte, Stephan Siegel, and Lance Young, subjects rated potential borrowers' trustworthiness after viewing photographs of them. It turned out that people who "look trustworthy" were more likely to have their loan requests granted. More surprisingly, they were also more likely to repay the loans. The implication was that if this type of fine-grained information could help market participants assess a transaction's prospects, it made sense to provide it.

On the websites of services ranging from freelancing to ride sharing to dog walking, many sellers now have discretion over whom they do business with on the basis of looks or even just a name. The availability of such information is platform-specific, with some sites preserving a fair amount of anonymity while others hark back to practices long banned in off-line markets. Similarly, on many sites, including Etsy and CustomMade, potential buyers see not only products but also the names and photos of sellers. Although having details about prospective transaction partners may make people more comfortable, a growing body of evidence shows that it facilitates discrimination.

The short-term-rental marketplace Airbnb is a case in point regarding the emergence of discrimination in online markets and the ways in which design choices influence the extent of it. When a would-be renter searches listings, he sees descriptions and pictures of both the property and the host. And hosts can see the names—and in many instances the pictures—of potential tenants before accepting or rejecting them.

One of us (Mike, working with Benjamin Edelman and Daniel Svirsky) has investigated racial discrimination on Airbnb. In a study focused on the U.S. market, the group constructed 20 user profiles and sent rental requests to roughly 6,400 hosts. The profiles and requests were identical except for one detail—the user's name. Half the profiles had names that (according to birth records) are common among whites, while half had names common among blacks.

Requests with black-sounding names were 16% less likely than those with white-sounding names to be accepted. And the discrimination was pervasive, occurring with cheap listings and expensive ones, diverse neighborhoods and homogeneous ones, rooms in the host's own dwelling and separate units rented out by landlords with multiple listings. Most of the hosts who declined requests from black-sounding profiles had never hosted a black guest—suggesting that some hosts are especially inclined to discriminate on the basis of race. (In response to this study and to a growing chorus of criticism from users and regulators, Airbnb commissioned a task force to identify ways to reduce discrimination, which proposed a series of changes in September 2016. We will discuss aspects of the announced policies below.)

Researchers have now documented racial discrimination in a variety of areas online, from labor markets to credit applications to housing. It is enabled by two features: markers of race, most obviously photographs but also subtler indicators, such as names; and discretion on the part of market participants over whom they transact with. As we will discuss in the next section, both are choices made by platform designers.

Another feature of online commerce has at times, also counterintuitively, nurtured rather than suppressed discrimination: the use of algorithms and big data. The search results Google serves up, the books Amazon suggests, and the movies Netflix recommends are all examples of machines' replacing imperfect human judgment about what customers want. It's tempting to assume that eliminating human judgment would eliminate human bias as well. But that's not the case.

In fact, algorithm-generated discrimination occurs in ways that humans would probably avoid. In an eye-opening study, computer science professor Latanya Sweeney sought to understand the role of race in Google ads. She searched for common African American names—such as Deshawn and, well, Latanya—and recorded the ads that appeared with the results. She then searched for names, such as Geoffrey, that are more common among whites. The searches for black-sounding names were more likely to generate ads offering to investigate possible arrest records.

Of course, Google didn't set out to show arrest-record ads to people who searched for African American names. That happened because an algorithm "decided," on the basis of past searches, that someone searching for "Deshawn" is more likely than someone searching for "Geoffrey" to click on an arrest-related ad (and hence generate revenue for Google). That is, the choice was made, if unwittingly, by Google's algorithm designers.

Toward Smarter Market Design

Platforms—even when they're in the same industry—often differ in their design features, which can lead to different levels of vulnerability to discrimination. Take the decision whether and when to post user pictures. Uber does not provide drivers with photos of potential passengers, but its competitor Lyft does. This makes Uber less vulnerable than Lyft to discrimination by drivers. Similarly, the main search-results page of the vacation rental marketplace HomeAway displays photos only of the property for rent and withholds host photos until a later page (if it shows them at all), whereas Airbnb requires that hosts include photos of themselves on its main search-results page.

Companies also have varying approaches to investigating possible discrimination and taking remedial action. For example, eBay worked with a team of social psychologists to explore whether male sellers get higher prices than female sellers for similar items (they do). More commonly, though, businesses avoid the issue. Although many executives acknowledge that discrimination occurs and express interest in reducing it, we've seen few earnest efforts like eBay's to gauge its extent. So researchers looking to study online discrimination must run their own experiments or scrape decidedly imperfect data from websites. (And we know of cases where company lawyers have gone after such efforts in an attempt to block race-related research.)

Even companies with the best of intentions may not choose the best approach to fighting discrimination, because, to our knowledge, no system exists for thinking through the available design choices and their implications. Our aim in what follows is to offer a framework for companies that want to design and manage a thriving marketplace while minimizing the risk of discrimination.

We don't expect every market designer to make the same decisions. Just as competitors make differing design choices about other situations (for instance, Lyft lets riders tip through its app, but Uber doesn't), they will make differing choices about confronting discrimination; among other reasons, they place differing premiums on avoiding discrimination (although we believe that platforms should hold themselves to a high standard in this regard). Our goal is to help designers fully consider the implications and trade-offs of their design choices.

Below we offer two guiding principles for platforms struggling with this market-design challenge. We then evaluate four design choices that are likely to affect discrimination.

Principle 1: Don't ignore the potential for discrimination

Platforms should start with more-careful tracking. Currently, most don't know the racial and gender composition of their transaction participants. A regular report (and an occasional audit) on the race and gender of users, along with measures of each group's success on the platform, is a necessary (though not sufficient) step toward revealing and confronting any problems. It can shed light on areas where discrimination is an issue and reveal progress over time. It can also be a good-faith first step toward reducing discrimination. For example, Airbnb should regularly report the acceptance rates of guests broken out by factors such as race and gender. Making this information public would help raise user and regulator awareness and keep pressure on companies to deal earnestly with discrimination problems that arise as their platforms evolve. (Public disclosure of discrimination-related data is one dimension on which Airbnb's announced policies fall far short—but it's needed to ensure that the company's broad, laudable goals translate into concrete results.)

Principle 2: Maintain an experimental mindset

Platforms should do what they do best—experiment. Companies including Facebook, Yelp, and eBay have baked experimental thinking into their development of new products and features. To test design choices that may, along with other interventions, influence the extent of discrimination, companies should conduct randomized controlled trials. Airbnb should be applauded for a recent experiment in withholding host photos from its main search-results page to explore the effects on booking outcomes (although it has not made the results public).

Design decision 1: Are you providing too much information?

In many cases, the simplest, most effective change a platform can make is to withhold potentially sensitive user information, such as race and gender, until after a transaction has been agreed to. Some platforms, including Amazon and eBay, already do this. For many others, however, it would mean departing from the way they do business. An executive of a platform with a billion-dollar valuation told us that his firm would never consider eliminating photos or names.

In addition to choosing what information to reveal, platforms choose how salient to make it. And a large body of evidence has shown that salience matters. On some platforms, for example, shipping costs are separate from—and less salient than—the base price. In an influential experiment, economists Jennifer Brown, Tanjim Hossain, and John Morgan demonstrated that in this situation, a lower base price increases the chance that an item will sell, even when it is offset by a higher shipping charge. In other words, a customer is influenced not only by the information he sees but also by which information is most prominent.

To see how this insight might be applied, recall the comparison of Airbnb, which displays host photos on its main search-results page, and HomeAway, which does not. (In September, Airbnb stated that it will test alternative ways of presenting photos and other race-relevant information, although it did not commit to specifics.) By reducing the salience of race, platforms could reduce discrimination.

Design decision 2: Could you further automate the transaction process?

When using Uber, you tap the screen to order a ride; only after confirming do you learn who will pick you up. In theory, you can then cancel if you don't like the driver's rating or looks. But that takes effort, and this small "transaction cost" is probably just enough to deter most looks-based cancellations. Uber could just as easily have allowed riders to see the driver before tapping confirm or cancel, but it chose not to.

Having transactions occur before race and gender are revealed makes it more difficult for people to discriminate. Consider the Airbnb feature known as "instant book," designed to make booking simpler and more convenient. A host using it allows renters to book her property without her having first approved them. Instant book is an opt-in feature: Landlords must sign up for it. Research has shown that default bias is strong: Most hosts will use whatever option is set up as the default. If Airbnb switched its default to instant book, requiring hosts to actively opt out of it, discrimination would most likely be lessened. The company might even consider making hosts pay for the privilege of screening customers—for example, it could charge a premium for opting out of instant book. (In September the company announced that it would accelerate the use of instant book, although it did not specify how it would accomplish this.)

We believe that increased automation and standard economic incentives, carefully implemented, could both reduce discrimination and—by eliminating some of the back-and-forth needed to complete a transaction—increase profits on a variety of platforms.

Design decision 3: Could you make discrimination policies more top-of-mind?

In a 2012 study, the research team of Lisa Shu, Nina Mazar, Francesca Gino, Dan Ariely, and Max Bazerman set out to test whether something as simple as the location of a signature on a form could affect honesty. They observed that people are often asked to fill out information and then sign at the end to attest to its veracity. They wondered whether people would be less likely to cheat if they signed at the very beginning of the form—before filling it out. Indeed, signing at the top led to less cheating in both a lab experiment and a real-world experiment with an auto insurance company. It also worked in the context of tax returns.

There's a lesson here for marketplaces: If you want people to do something, think carefully about when to prompt them. Most platforms have policies prohibiting discrimination, but they're buried in fine print. For example, Airbnb hosts must agree not to discriminate—but they do so when first signing up to be a landlord. By the time a host is deciding whether to accept a potential renter, she has probably forgotten that agreement. Marketplaces could present antidiscrimination policies at a more relevant moment—and have the host's agreement not to discriminate occur during the actual transaction process. Some people would still violate the policies, of course, but that would require a much more conscious choice.

Design decision 4: Should your algorithms be discrimination-aware?

Design choices also determine the extent to which an algorithm leads to discrimination. Thus far many algorithm designers have ignored factors such as race and gender and just hoped for the best. But in many cases the probability that an algorithm will unintentionally achieve equality is essentially zero; recall how Google's algorithms handled ads for arrest records.

If an algorithm designer cares about fairness, she needs to track how race or gender impacts the user experience and to set explicit objectives. Does she want to ensure that black customers are not rejected at higher rates than white customers? That women are offered the same prices as men?

Google tweaked its algorithm in response to the arrest-record study, but companies can proactively monitor and respond to such problems. That might entail compensating for some users' discrimination. For example, suppose Uber noticed that some passengers consistently gave low ratings to black drivers who received five stars from most of their other riders. The company could underweight ratings from those passengers—who have revealed themselves to be discriminatory—when calculating black drivers' overall feedback scores.

A Lesson from Symphony Orchestras

Platforms exist within a larger social context, of course; we can't create a color- and gender-blind world simply by designing platforms that are less apt to facilitate discrimination. And it would be wishful thinking to imagine that every platform designer aspired to that goal; sometimes enabling discrimination is good for business. When that's the case, we can only appeal to business leaders' sense of social responsibility or hope that government regulation will intervene.

But there are many instances in which the idea of "doing well by doing good" does hold—times when platform businesses could reduce discrimination at a low cost or even while increasing profits. It's also possible that a few enlightened businesses could start a virtual cycle that forces better behavior from other market participants.

Consider how the challenge of creating diversity in U.S. symphony orchestras was met. In the mid-1960s, less than 10% of the musicians in the "big five" U.S. orchestras (Boston, Philadelphia,

Chicago, New York, and Cleveland) were women. In the 1970s and 1980s, as part of a broader diversity initiative, the groups changed their audition procedures to eliminate potential bias. Instead of conducting auditions face-to-face, they seated musicians behind a screen or other divider. In a landmark 2000 study, economists Claudia Goldin and Cecilia Rouse found that the screen increased the success rate of female musicians by 160%. In fact, they attributed roughly a quarter of the orchestras' increased gender diversity to this simple change. And with selection based more squarely on musical ability, the orchestras were undoubtedly better off.

When we first read this study, many years ago, we were intrigued by the rare glimpse it provided into discrimination's effects and by the outsize impact of a small change. But the solution felt frustratingly context-specific. It was hard to imagine gender- or race-blind interactions between buyers and sellers or employers and job candidates.

The online era has changed that. Early on we witnessed the internet's potential to create marketplaces free of race, gender, and age considerations. We've now evolved far enough that platform designers can choose where and when to place virtual screens. We hope they will use that power to create a more inclusive society.

Originally published in December 2016. Reprint R1612G

RON ADNER is a professor of strategy and entrepreneurship at Dartmouth College's Tuck School of Business. In his book *The Wide Lens: What Successful Innovators See That Others Miss*, he introduces a new approach to ecosystem strategy.

ELIZABETH J. ALTMAN is an assistant professor of strategic management at the Manning School of Business at the University of Massachusetts Lowell and a visiting scholar at Harvard Business School. She was formerly a vice president of strategy and business development at Motorola.

SANGEET PAUL CHOUDARY advises executives globally on platform business models and is an entrepreneur-in-residence at INSEAD. He has been ranked among the top 30 emerging global business thinkers by Thinkers50 and selected as a Young Global Leader by the World Economic Forum. He is a coauthor (with Geoffrey G. Parker and Marshall W. Van Alstyne) of *Platform Revolution* (W.W. Norton & Company, 2016).

BENJAMIN EDELMAN is an economist at Microsoft.

THOMAS EISENMANN is the Howard H. Stevenson Professor of Business Administration at the Harvard Business School and a cochair of the Rock Center for Entrepreneurship.

RAY FISMAN is the Slater Family Professor in Behavioral Economics at Boston University and a coauthor of *The Inner Lives of Markets: How People Shape Them—and They Shape Us* (PublicAffairs, 2016).

DAMIEN GERADIN is a professor at Tilburg University, as well as the founding partner of EDGE Legal, a Brussels-based law firm specializing in EU competition law and intellectual property law.

ANDREI HAGIU is an associate professor of information systems at Boston University's Questrom School of Business.

MARCO IANSITI is the David Sarnoff Professor of Business Administration at Harvard Business School, where he heads the Technology and Operations Management Unit and the Digital Initiative. He has advised many companies in the technology sector, including Microsoft, Facebook, and Amazon. He is a coauthor of the book *Competing in the Age of AI* (Harvard Business Review Press, 2020).

MICHAEL G. JACOBIDES holds the Sir Donald Gordon Chair for Entrepreneurship and Innovation at the London Business School.

RAHUL KAPOOR is an associate professor of management at the Wharton School. His research focuses on managing industry disruption and business ecosystems from the perspective of both established and emerging firms.

KARIM R. LAKHANI is the Charles Edward Wilson Professor of Business Administration and the Dorothy and Michael Hintze Fellow at Harvard Business School and the founder and a codirector of the Laboratory for Innovation Science at Harvard. He is a coauthor (with Marco Iansiti) of the book *Competing in the Age of AI* (Harvard Business Review Press, 2020).

MICHAEL LUCA is the Lee J. Styslinger III Associate Professor of Business Administration at Harvard Business School and a coauthor (with Max H. Bazerman) of *The Power of Experiments: Decision-Making in a Data-Driven World* (MIT Press, 2020).

GEOFFREY G. PARKER is a professor of engineering at Dartmouth College and a research fellow at MIT's Initiative on the Digital Economy. He coauthored (with Marshall W. Van Alstyne and Sangeet Paul Choudary) *Platform Revolution* (W.W. Norton & Company, 2016).

SIMON ROTHMAN is a partner at Greylock Partners. He was formerly the head of operations at eBay and founded eBay Motors. He has served as an adviser to a number of startups, including Lyft, TaskRabbit, Tango, and Fiverr.

MARSHALL W. VAN ALSTYNE is the Questrom Chaired Professor at Boston University School of Business. His work has more than 10,000 citations. He coauthored (with Geoffrey G. Parker and Sangeet Paul Choudary) *Platform Revolution* (W.W. Norton & Company, 2016).

DAVID B. YOFFIE is the Max and Doris Starr Professor of International Business Administration at Harvard Business School. He is a coauthor of *The Business of Platforms: Strategy in the Age of Digital Competition, Innovation and Power* (HarperBusiness, 2019).

MING ZENG is the chairman of the Academic Council of the Alibaba Group, an e-commerce, retail, and technology conglomerate, based in Hangzhou, China, and the author of *Smart Business: What Alibaba's Success Reveals About the Future of Strategy* (Harvard Business Review Press, 2018). He is also the dean of Hupan School of Entrepreneurship, a private business school founded by Alibaba chairman Jack Ma and other leading Chinese entrepreneurs in Hangzhou.

FENG ZHU is the Piramal Associate Professor of Business Administration at Harvard Business School. He studies competitive strategy and innovation in high-technology industries, with an emphasis on platform-based markets.

Index

Engage with HBR content the way you want, on any device.

With HBR's new subscription plans, you can access world-renowned **case studies** from Harvard Business School and receive **four free eBooks**. Download and customize prebuilt **slide decks and graphics** from our **Visual Library**. With HBR's archive, top 50 best-selling articles, and five new articles every day, HBR is more than just a magazine.

Subscribe Today
hbr.org/success

The most important management ideas all in one place.

We hope you enjoyed this book from *Harvard Business Review*. Now you can get even more with HBR's 10 Must Reads Boxed Set. From books on leadership and strategy to managing yourself and others, this 6-book collection delivers articles on the most essential business topics to help you succeed.

HBR's 10 Must Reads Series

The definitive collection of ideas and best practices on our most sought-after topics from the best minds in business.

- Change Management
- Collaboration
- Communication
- Emotional Intelligence
- Innovation
- Leadership
- Making Smart Decisions

- Managing Across Cultures
- Managing People
- Managing Yourself
- Strategic Marketing
- Strategy
- Teams
- The Essentials

hbr.org/mustreads

Buy for your team, clients, or event.
Visit hbr.org/bulksales for quantity discount rates.

Harvard
Business
Review
Press